NOT-SO-NICE B

GORY DEATHS

Written by Jonathan Schkade   Illustrated by Maisson Cipriano

CONCORDIA PUBLISHING HOUSE · SAINT LOUIS

This book was written in remembrance of all the faithful
who endured suffering for the sake of the cross. As they now
see God face-to-face, so, too, may we.

Published by Concordia Publishing House
3558 S. Jefferson Avenue, St. Louis, MO 63118-3968
1-800-325-3040 · www.cph.org

Manufactured in the United States of America

1 2 3 4 5 6 7 8 9 10   25 24 23 22 21 20 19 18 17 16

INTRODUCTION

By now you've read the title of this book, so you know this isn't going to be a jolly, Mary Poppins–ish romp through the pages of the Bible. There are no dancing penguins, no laugh-filled tea parties, and no friendly chimney sweeps covered in soot—though soot itself may appear more than once.

Instead, this book will yank away your spoonful of sugar and give you the medicine of truth, bitter and harsh. This is a book about death, but not just any deaths are included. Oh no. These pages discuss many of the least pleasant, most brutal, and outright goriest deaths recorded in the Bible. They are definitely not hidden or tidied up.

A word of caution: if you're looking to be grossed out purely for the fun of it, this is not the right book for you. While the lethal part of each story will be the focus, that's not all you will find. Contained here also are heroes and villains, opportunities and obstacles, failures and faith-building lessons for us all.

So, why these stories? There are countless books focusing on biblical accounts that are grand, heroic, and joyful. Good. From such books you can learn many things. Here, though, you see people at their worst: sinful, sinister, and sneaky. From them, you can learn much about what not to do and about repenting from similar sins you already commit. You can see the full weight of God's justice smashing evil, and you can resolve to not let evil have any foothold in your life.

More than that, through these true histories you'll see God in action, saving the helpless who are oppressed and pouring out mercy to people based not on their power or possessions but on humility and faith in Him.

You can view the gory deaths covered in this book as fulfilling one of two purposes: (1) executing judgment upon sin or (2) giving hope and deliverance to those who trust in the Lord. And, yes, some do both. As you read, think about and question the words of this book and consider for yourself the purpose of each story here and in the Bible. God didn't include them there on a whim. He had truth to impart and lessons to lay out. This book attempts to help you see more clearly what God has placed before you. Consider how you might fit into each story and how sin always condemns you, while God's gift of Jesus always frees you.

There were seldom people less worthy of God's love and forgiveness than the bulk of the people whose deaths you'll read about in this book. But even these people were not beyond God's power to save. With each story, ponder that great what-if of repentance. Think through how so many of these deaths and lives would have changed if the people who died had sought God's mercy, prayed to Him in faith, and received His unending love.

One last note: this is not a book of fairy tales or fiction. Happy endings are few and far-between. This is, however, a book of history, recounting true tales of people who lived long ago in a world filled with people much like us. Embrace their stories as tools for shaping the story of your life as God guides you in the days, months, and years to come.

CHAPTER 1

LET IT BRIMSTONE!

Who died: People of Sodom and Gomorrah / Lot's wife

How they died: Sulfur and fire from heaven / turned into a pillar of salt

Why they died: Evil and immorality / disobedience

When: 2067 BC, shortly before the founding of Egypt's Middle Kingdom and around the time that China's first dynasty, the Xia dynasty, was founded

Where in Scripture: Genesis 18–19

God's a real killjoy, isn't He? Sodom and Gomorrah, cities full of people in a valley full of people that God annihilates just because He can. It's not like they were oppressing anyone, let alone God's people. They were welcoming to Lot and his family. They're not even like other people in the Bible who blocked the way of the children of Israel's resettlement. God destroyed them for one main reason: they were wicked to the core.

Modern smarties would say, "Yeah, but how was that God's business? They weren't bugging Him. He shouldn't have bugged them." But that's the point. Everything that everyone everywhere does is God's business, and evil stinking to high heaven is not something God ignores. Evil breeds evil. Corruption breeds corruption. As the one who sees across centuries, God knew their evil would spread over time, as, indeed, it already had to Lot and his family. First, though, let's backtrack to Abraham and his game of *Let's Make a Deal* with God.

LET'S MAKE A DEAL

It should have been good times for Abraham. God and a couple of angels had visited him personally, enjoyed his hospitality, and promised the old man and his old wife a son within the year. Impossible, incredible, undeniable joy. It's no wonder Abraham wanted to hang out with the visitors a bit. Who knew what other surprises God might have for him? As it turns out, what awaited him was a far less welcome surprise. God gave Abraham the heads-up that He was planning to inspect and, if He was displeased, destroy the cities of Sodom and Gomorrah, as well as the whole valley. Wouldn't you know it? Sodom was exactly where Abraham's nephew Lot lived. It was time to make a deal.

Knowing that Sodom was a big place, and not caring a whiff about Gomorrah or the rest of the valley, Abraham started with a generous but, he thought, practical opening number: fifty. He asked God, "What if there are fifty righteous people in Sodom? Surely You wouldn't destroy all those good people just to get at a few troublemakers? Surely You are a just Judge." Abraham laid it on as thick as peanut butter.

Perhaps to Abraham's surprise, God agreed. "Sure, if there are fifty, I'll leave the town alone."

Just like a used-car salesman, Abraham was already thinking, *Wow, that was easy. I should have started lower.* "How about for-ty-five?" he countered.

JUST WONDERING: DO OUR REQUESTS AFFECT GOD'S ACTIONS? IF SO, HOW? SEE 1 SAMUEL 1; 2 KINGS 20:1–11; AND EXODUS 32:1–14 FOR MORE INPUT.

God again said yes, and before a guy could blink, Abraham pled and prodded his way down to forty, thirty, twenty, and finally ten. Why he didn't go for a final four, the number of people in Lot's immediate family, and really lock it in, who can say. Perhaps he realized he'd reached the limit of God's patience. Perhaps he thought about the whole world being destroyed in the flood, even though there were eight people aboard the ark. Perhaps he thought ten was enough. Surely, in a town that size, there would be ten righteous people.

Regardless, the deal was struck, and the two angels disguised as men headed into Sodom for the evening to check things out.

MEET THE MOB

When the two "men" got to Sodom, who should they meet by the city gate but Lot himself. Lot had no doubt been chatting and doing business with his neighbors, perhaps coming up with new ways to expand his wealth. Right about now in the story, we get Lot at his high point from a materialistic perspective. Having chosen the lush Jordan Valley for his flocks and herds, Lot was surely prospering (Genesis 13). And he lounged in a comfy spot in the gate, a position of power and privilege.

This was also Lot's high point as a person of good character, as he insisted on inviting the two strangers into his house for the night. In that part of the world and at that time in history, this was the right way to treat guests— even if they were complete strangers. Only God knows if Lot was solely focused on the hosting tradition or if he was also thinking about what might happen if they spent the night in the streets of that wicked city. Either way, they came home with him, scarfed down a good supper, and were all set for bed. That's when the yelling started.

THAT REMINDS ME: "DO NOT NEGLECT TO SHOW HOSPITALITY TO STRANGERS, FOR THEREBY SOME HAVE ENTERTAINED ANGELS UNAWARES." HEBREWS 13:2

You've all seen movies where a mob surrounds someone's house, revved up for violence and in no mood for an argument. That's what Lot faced. And this was some mob—every man in the city, young and old. Together they yelled for him to send out the two honored visitors so they could use them and abuse them. Essentially, they wanted to molest these men. There's no way Lot would go along with this, was there?

At first, Lot looked every bit the hero, stepping outside the house, facing the crowd of men, and commanding them, "Do not act so wickedly" (Genesis 19:7). But just when you're impressed with Lot's courage and holiness, he opens his mouth again: "Behold, I have two daughters who have not known any man. Let me bring them out to you, and do to them as you please. Only do nothing to these men, for they have come under the shelter of my roof" (v. 8).

THAT REMINDS ME: JUDGES 19 (ESPECIALLY VV. 16–30) SHARES THE ACCOUNT OF A TRAVELING LEVITE AND HIS CONCUBINE—A FEMALE SLAVE AND SORT-OF JUNIOR WIFE—WHO RECEIVE A WELCOME MUCH LIKE THAT GIVEN TO LOT'S GUESTS. BEWARE! THIS STORY IS NOT FOR THE FAINT OF HEART.

Not exactly father-of-the-year material. Can you imagine how Lot's daughters, trembling inside the house, felt when they heard their father offer them as sacrifices to the mob of crazed men? Fortunately for them, the crowd rejected Lot's offer. In that instant, Lot went from a valued member of the community to a despised newcomer. As the crowd rose up against Lot and prepared to beat down the door, Lot's odds of a happy ending tanked. By the end of the night, he would likely be dead, and his family and guests sorely abused, beaten, and possibly killed themselves.

THE ANGELS TAKE CHARGE

Seconds later, Lot's lot had changed a lot. The angel guests stuck their hands outside and yanked Lot back in. Then, to end the immediate danger, they struck the men of the mob with blindness and confusion so that they exhausted themselves, unable to find the door.

But the angels knew it was no time to relax. That's when they dropped the bomb on Lot: "God sent us to wipe out this place because the people's acts are so evil it's like they're screaming for God to punish them." They sent Lot out to grab his daughters' fiancés so they could all leave the city together. His potential sons-in-law, though, laughed it off as one of Papa Lot's jokes.

After a long night, the angels bugged Lot to get his family out of there pronto, before the destruction came. "But he lingered" (19:16). Lingered? The wrath of heaven was about to rain down, and Lot lingered. Perhaps he liked his house too much or hated leaving his valuables and flocks behind. Perhaps he thought the night before was a fluke and he and his neighbors would be buddies again soon. Whatever his thinking, it was flat out idiotic.

JUST WONDERING: GENESIS 19:4 SAYS ALL THE MEN OF THE CITY WERE IN THE LUST-CRAZED MOB. DOES THAT MEAN IT INCLUDED THESE FIANCÉS? IF SO, WHAT DOES IT SAY ABOUT LOT THAT HE WAS STILL WILLING TO BRING THEM ALONG?

The angels thought so too, because they grabbed the hands of Lot, his wife, and his two daughters and dragged them out of the city. There, the angels gave them God's command: "Run for your lives and don't look back! Head for the hills or you'll be destroyed too!"

It's seems that Lot, though, was born with the same bargaining gene as Uncle Abraham. "Thanks, but the hills are sooooo far away. Can't we head for an itty-bitty town nearby instead? It's so tiny. You can spare that place too, right?"

Perhaps sighing, God agreed to spare the "itty-bitty" town of Zoar so Lot wouldn't have to go all the way to the hills that day—even though not much later Lot headed for the hills anyway.

HELL ON EARTH

Hellfire and brimstone, that is. As the Bible puts it, as soon as Lot reached Zoar, "the LORD rained on Sodom and Gomorrah sulfur and fire from the LORD out of heaven" (19:24). Nothing and no one survived. The cities, the valley, the people, the plants on the ground—all of it was obliterated. Some suggest God used an earthquake to release deadly gases into the air. Others spin tales of pieces of a comet or an asteroid slamming into the earth. God could use whatever method He wanted, including something we can't naturally explain.

The Bible itself says sulfur—a.k.a. brimstone—and fire, making it clear that the people burned and endured foul air. Some may have died from the fire falling from the sky, burning them alive or driving straight through flesh and bone. Being inside a dwelling wouldn't have helped. They didn't have fire safety drills back then, and there were no long red trucks speeding to the rescue. Anyone not immediately consumed by flames would have choked on the smoke. You've likely smelled sulfur—whether in a science class or near a rotten egg or a skunk's stench. Crank that up a hundred times over. In Sodom and Gomorrah, lungs filled with this noxious gas, smoke from the fires all around, and ashes from everything else burning. Breathing would have been impossible, perhaps a mercy before the fire burned everyone to ashes. Or, if the people of Sodom were really lucky, the heat might have killed them all in an instant.

Sodom and Gomorrah were destroyed. Lot and his family were saved. The story should be over, but it's not.

THAT REMINDS ME: THE PEOPLE OF SODOM AND GOMORRAH DID NOT KNOW THE END WAS COMING FOR THEM, MUCH LIKE WHAT CHRIST SAYS ABOUT HIS RETURN IN MATTHEW 24:36–44.

LICKED BY SALT

God gave one command to Lot's family on their escape route: "Don't look back." Such a simple direction. So easy to follow. God had saved the family from certain destruction. You'd think they could follow one little command.

It's not so easy after all. Try this for the next few minutes: don't look at your feet. That's right, no matter what, do not look at your feet. It shouldn't be hard. You don't have a shoelace untied or anything. Still, by this point, some of you have already glanced down or at least had to focus extra hard not to do it. That's because people are contrary by nature. We want to do whatever we're told not to do. It's instinct.

So, Lot's wife turning around for one last look at Sodom shouldn't be a surprise. Not only was God's command echoing in her head, taunting her, but this was her home. It was where everything and everyone she loved, apart from her children and husband, remained. The truly astounding detail is that Lot and their daughters didn't look back as well.

Was it willful disobedience that made her turn? Weak-willed curiosity? A need to lock the memory of the town in her mind? It doesn't matter. What matters is that God gave a command, and she disobeyed. It's hard for us to understand how this tiny sin deserved a death penalty. The truth is, though, that every sin earns death. One sin, no matter how small, is enough to violate God's Law, making us no longer holy, no longer worthy of eternal life with God. It is up to God to judge such things, not us. And so, this woman identified only by her husband's name, was turned into a pillar of salt. Ancient writers said that her salty monument remained visible still, even centuries later, as a reminder not to turn back from God's path, not to seek even a glimpse of the evil lives from which Christ has called us.

Did she burn from the inside out? Was she wrapped in dust and pummeled to powder? Were her cells transformed instantly into salt? Regardless, it was a horrific fate. And while we're told that she was behind Lot, it must have been a chilling moment for her daughters. Either she was in front of them and they saw what happened when she turned back, or she was behind them and they knew only that she was suddenly silent. If she was behind them, they couldn't have turned to check on her without suffering the same fate. Imagine such a thing happening to your own mother. The memory would never go away.

So, the story ends with Lot and his daughters safe in Zoar, Lot's wife a pillar of salt, and thousands of people burned to noth- ingness. This takes place in a region we now know as the Dead Sea, a place where little grows, and the water is so salty no fish can survive. So much destruction, but we are reminded at the end that "God remembered Abraham and sent Lot out of the midst of the overthrow" (19:29). Mercy even then.

JUST WONDERING: COULD THE DEATH OF LOT'S WIFE HAVE BEEN AN ACT OF MERCY? HOW?

WHY IS THIS IN THE BIBLE?

There's stuff that's bad.

There's stuff that's evil.

And then there's Sodom and Gomorrah.

Sodom and Gomorrah really were hell on earth in a lot of ways, especially when we think of hell the way the Bible does: separation from God. Through intentional repeated acts of evil, the people there separated themselves from God. Sin moves us away from God's will, God's love, and God's presence. When done again and again without repentance, sin moves us so far from God that even our consciences stop whispering to us the difference between right and wrong.

This is an idea we'll visit repeatedly in this book. It's certainly a good reason for this story to be in Scripture. God warns us about the potential consequences of our sinful actions, both the long-standing, repeated sins of the people of Sodom and Gomorrah and the single deadly choice made by Lot's wife. There's no such thing as a meaningless sin. God calls us to be attentive to all our choices, both big and small.

This true Bible story falls in a tradition of events where the sinful pride of human beings was punished by God. In the days of Noah, all people but

Noah and his family were destroyed. At the Tower of Babel, the people's language was confused, and they were spread out across the earth. And then we have Sodom.

From the tale of Sodom and Gomorrah, we learn much of God's need for justice. Sin must be punished. We also learn of His patience and willingness to show mercy to those who trust Him. Lot is not the greatest role model, and Abraham's wheeling and dealing with God doesn't seem like the most trusting behavior. But God doesn't show mercy because we have earned it, just like He takes no joy in passing judgment. God passes judgment because it must be done, because if He doesn't punish sin, sin will destroy every person everywhere. That's also why He shows mercy. If He didn't, sin and God's holy judgment upon it would destroy us forever. Wherever He sees a glimmer of hope that we might continue believing in Him, God casts us a line to grab onto. For Abraham's sake, He cast such a line to Lot. For Christ's sake, who pled with God for mercy with His own blood, He casts a line to us.

One more thought about these events: just a few chapters earlier, in Genesis 14, Abraham, with the help of God, rescued Lot and many citizens of Sodom and the surrounding area from an alliance of kings. He defeated the combined army and delivered back to the king of Sodom all that had been taken. God had already shown mercy to the people of Sodom and Gomorrah, yet they continued in their wickedness.

BONUS FEATURES

Speaking of Sodom and Gomorrah: Divine destruction on the scale of Sodom and Gomorrah doesn't happen every day. The cities' wicked reputation and fiery finish endured in the minds of the Jewish people for generation after generation. With more than twenty references outside of Genesis, this is one of the most referred-to events in the Bible. God clearly intended the annihilation of Sodom to stand as a warning against unbridled sin. One unflinching example is 2 Peter 2:6: "By turning the cities of Sodom and Gomorrah to ashes He condemned them to extinction, making them an example of what is going to happen to the ungodly."

Salty sayings: Prized for thousands of years as a preservative, flavoring, and essential part of the diet, salt has inspired numerous words and phrases, including these:

> *Salary:* Salt-money, the wage Roman soldiers were paid to buy salt
> *The salt of the earth:* The best people
> *Worth your salt:* You're good at what you do
> *Take with a grain of salt:* Be very skeptical
> *An old salt:* A sailor or a teller of sea stories

Civic destruction: Although Sodom and Gomorrah own a unique reputation as subjects of God's wrath, countless other cities have suffered unexpected devastation over the centuries. Here are a few that stand out for the speed, severity, and shocking nature of their destruction.

Pompeii: Along with the nearby city of Herculaneum, Pompeii and its approximately twenty thousand residents were erased from history in AD 79, when the Mt. Vesuvius volcano erupted. Those who didn't choke to death on ash were hit by volcanic rock, crushed by ash-laden roofs, or killed by inescapable surges of superheated poison gas, which either suffocated them or shocked them to death with its intense heat. Pompeii was forgotten until its rediscovery in 1748. Ash preserved whole buildings, household tools, and skeletons frozen in life's last moments.

Helike: In 373 BC, the citizens of the ancient Greek city of Helike were confused as for five days snakes, rats, and other critters fled the city as fast as their little bellies and legs could take them. On the fifth day, massive columns of flame, now known as earthquake lights, flashed in the sky. That was the final warning. When the quake hit, there was no time for the people to escape. The sandy ground beneath the city liquefied—think mega-size quicksand—and sucked the city downward below sea level. The city collapsed and chunks of land fell into the sea, which may have triggered a huge wave known as a tsunami. This massive wave raced across the Gulf of Corinth, rebounded off the opposite coast, and came rushing back to flood the sunken city. Some say the legend of Atlantis is based on this event.

Port Royal: Pirates took a major blow in 1692 when the Jamaican town of Port Royal slid beneath the ocean in a Helike-like disaster. This booming home to pirates, merchants, and people of low repute was often called the Sodom of the New World. Unfortunately for its residents, the city was foolishly planned and constructed. The English residents of this originally Spanish town built heavy brick structures on a foundation that was essentially wet sand. It was like the parable from Matthew 7:24–27 acted out. Within two minutes of the earthquake and accompanying tsunami, 90 percent of the city was underwater, almost as if it had melted away. Three thousand people, roughly half the population, died and two thousand more died from disease in the aftermath.

CHAPTER 2

A Plague by Any Other Name Would Still Stink

Who died: Many animals, Egyptians, and the firstborn sons of Egypt

How they died: Various plagues

Why they died: Pride and hard-heartedness of Pharaoh

When: 1447–1446 BC, not long after the last of the Minoan civilization was destroyed

Where in Scripture: Exodus 7–12

What's in a heart? We know our brains do the thinking, and our emotions have little to do with the beating muscle that pumps blood through the body. But as poets and love-smitten souls everywhere know, there's more to the heart than biology.

To the Egyptians and many in the ancient world, the heart, not the brain, did the heavy lifting. The heart thought and planned and felt, and it was linked forever to the soul.

The ancient Egyptians reflected this belief in their practice of leaving the heart in the body during the mummification process. Most of the other organs were pulled out and put in jars. The brain was swished up with a long hook and thrown away. The heart, they thought, would be useful in the afterlife. According to their religion, the dead people's hearts would be weighed to determine their eternal fate. Those heavy-hearted souls guilty of wrongdoing would have their hearts eaten and they would be cast into darkness, and those light-hearted innocent souls would go to paradise.

The irony of this was certainly lost on the pharaoh who ruled at the time of Moses. Pharaoh (a title, not a name) is described as hard-hearted over and over again in Exodus. This man had a heart so weighed down with cruelty that it never would have passed the test of his own false deities. The true God of the universe was even less impressed.

THAT REMINDS ME: "I WILL GIVE YOU A NEW HEART, AND A NEW SPIRIT I WILL PUT WITHIN YOU. AND I WILL REMOVE THE HEART OF STONE FROM YOUR FLESH AND GIVE YOU A HEART OF FLESH." EZEKIEL 36:26

PLAGUE PRELUDE

Ever since Joseph welcomed his brothers' families to Egypt four centuries earlier, Israel's descendants had prospered and multiplied among the Egyptians. Over time, Joseph's invaluable service to the Egyptians was forgotten. As a result, the children of Israel went from a blessing to a burden in the eyes of the Egyptian leadership. They went from guests to slaves.

Although the Egyptians tried to kill the male Hebrew babies to prevent the slave population from growing strong, their plan failed, and the children of Israel increased in strength and number. And not only was a tiny baby named Moses saved from death, but he was adopted by Pharaoh's daughter too. God's hand was at work putting the pieces in place for the next chapter of history.

While Moses grew, the Hebrew people suffered under the increasing demands of Pharaoh's taskmasters. Moses murdered an abusive Egyptian, fled from Egypt, and married. Meanwhile, one king of Egypt died and another took power, and the Hebrew people's cries for freedom continued.

Determined not to leave the people of Israel in slavery, God appeared in a burning bush to Moses and called him to return to Egypt so he could lead them to their new home in the Promised Land. Moses fussed and fretted, but God would not be swayed, so Moses agreed to go before Pharaoh as long as his brother Aaron came along. Together, they would announce God's demand for His people's freedom.

> **THAT REMINDS ME:** GOD DIDN'T USE ONLY A SINGLE METHOD TO SPEAK TO HIS SERVANTS IN THE OLD TESTAMENT. READ 1 KINGS 19 TO DISCOVER HOW GOD REVEALED HIMSELF TO ELIJAH.

WHY SO MANY PLAGUES?

Before we dig in, let's face it: ten plagues seem like a lot. Why did our merciful God dump out plague after plague upon all the people and animals of Egypt? Since God knew it would take the tenth plague to convince Pharaoh to let God's people go, why all the build-up? Why not send just that one and skip the rest?

The answer is that God is always eager to make it possible for us to avoid the worst fate. It's in His nature to give us numerous chances to hear and receive His Word. Even though He knows every answer that will ever be given, He does not casually remove our opportunities to believe what He has said.

In Pharaoh's case, each plague was an opportunity to repent, to respect God's authority, and to honor God's demands. Belief and true, heart-deep repentance at any point would have eliminated the need for any further plagues. That's the chance God offered Pharaoh by not just skipping to plague number 10, by far the worst of the lot.

Each plague was both a judgment upon Pharaoh and a shot at claiming mercy. God didn't want to kill anyone. He didn't want to inflict ten plagues to get Pharaoh to release his grip. That was Pharaoh's stubborn choice, not God's.

WARMING UP

In their first crack at Pharaoh, Moses and Aaron simply asked to travel a few days into the wilderness to have a feast in God's honor. Pharaoh answered, "God who? I don't know this God, so forget about it." And just to make it clear that time off from work wasn't going to happen, he took away the straw the people of Israel needed to make bricks. This increased their workload significantly.

Now the true battle of wills began, not between Pharaoh and Moses, but between Pharaoh and God. In our eyes, this was an unfair battle. But as far as Pharaoh was concerned, a great line of Egyptian gods had his back. What's more, Pharaoh considered himself more of a god-king than a mere man. He was not about to let some new deity on the block get in his way.

JUST WONDERING: GOD COULD HAVE FORCED MOSES TO APPROACH PHARAOH ON HIS OWN. WHY DID HE ALLOW AARON TO GO ALONG AND TO SPEAK AND ACT AS A MIDDLEMAN BETWEEN MOSES AND PHARAOH? HOW DID THIS TIE IN TO AARON'S LATER JOB AS HIGH PRIEST OF ISRAEL?

When Aaron turned his staff into a snake, Pharaoh practically rolled his eyes and waved to his magicians. They, either through trickery or the limited power of Satan, copied Aaron, turning staffs into snakes. Never mind that Aaron's snake ate all of theirs; Pharaoh was not impressed and his heart was hardened.

FIRST THREE INNINGS

Moses and Aaron ambushed Pharaoh at the Nile River and laid God's words out straight: "Since you did not let My people worship Me, I'll show you I'm the Lord." Aaron stretched out his staff and struck the water. Instantly, the water of the Nile turned to blood, as did all the water connected to it, be it canals, ponds, or pools of water.

This, like all the plagues, was not just a warning and judgment upon Pharaoh. It was also judgment upon the false gods of Egypt. Each plague undermined the supposed power of at least one of the Egyptian gods. Here, God started by defeating the river gods. Systematically, God took on the deities of Egypt, proving them to be powerless—and, as we know, nonexistent—before Him.

The Nile's fish, of course, died, and as everyone knows about dead fish, they stink! Egypt was literally soaked in blood, so the people could not drink from their main water source. Plus, rotting fish floated in the river, canals, and ponds. But Pharaoh's magicians managed to imitate this miracle as well, so Pharaoh remained hard-hearted. For seven days, the people had to dig near the Nile to find anything clean enough to drink.

Scholars debate whether the Nile water was literally turned into blood or whether God enhanced a natural algae bloom way beyond the norm. Either way, this was no ordinary event, and it would never have happened without divine intervention.

> **THAT REMINDS ME:** JESUS' FIRST MIRACLE IN THE NEW TESTAMENT WAS STRIKINGLY SIMILAR TO THE FIRST PLAGUE. IN THE PLAGUE, THE WATER WAS TURNED INTO SOMETHING HARMFUL. BUT AT THE WEDDING AT CANA, JESUS TURNED THE WATER INTO SOMETHING PLEASING: WINE.

Before the second plague, team Yahweh (Moses and Aaron), went to Pharaoh again with the command to let His people go or else. This time, the promised "or else" was a plague of frogs. Pharaoh didn't budge, so Aaron pointed his staff, and presto, an army of frogs invaded the houses of Egypt. They were everywhere—in beds, ovens, bowls, and sitting on people's heads no doubt!

While those sneaky magicians copied this plague too, they had no clue how to get rid of the frogs, so Pharaoh begged Moses and Aaron to pray for God to remove the hopping horrors. Pharaoh promised that if they did, he would let Israel go to the wilderness to sacrifice to their God. Moses, being a nice guy and all, said, "Sure, just tell me when, and God will clear them out." Moses prayed, God killed the frogs, and the people gathered up huge frog

piles throughout the land. Much like the dead fish, this did not leave a good scent. But at least Pharaoh had given in, right? Not so much. Once he saw that the problem was gone, the nasty king changed his mind.

Up to this point, Pharaoh felt at least somewhat in control. He was receiving warnings before the bad stuff happened, and his mighty magicians had imitated the wonders of the God of Israel every step of the way. It was no doubt disturbing, then, when the next plague hit without any warning from Moses and Aaron. Gnats swarmed from the dust, covering man and animal alike, and likely inflicting painful bites.

JUST WONDERING: SINCE THE NILE HAD ALREADY BEEN TURNED INTO BLOOD AND GOD HAD ALREADY FILLED THE LAND WITH FROGS, WHAT DID THE MAGICIANS' "REPLICATION" OF THESE MIGHTY ACTS LOOK LIKE? DID THEY MATCH THE POWER OF THE ORIGINALS?

Worse yet, the magicians couldn't begin to replicate these pests. From here on, their power was broken. No more plagues could be copied by their evil arts. They knew it too, for they said to Pharaoh, "This is the finger of God" (Exodus 8:19). The proof was undeniable that Pharaoh, his magicians, and their false gods were in over their heads. Pharaoh, nevertheless, doubled down on stoniness. He was not about to listen to these hated foreigners and their God.

FOUR THROUGH SIX GIVE THEIR LICKS

Moses and Aaron repeated God's command again without luck, leading God to send suffocating swarms of flies throughout the homes and land of the Egyptians. This time, however, instead of the people of Israel sharing in the agony, God spared them. The land of Goshen, the area where Israel lived, was free of flies. Here, too, a new pattern began where a plague would strike Egypt, but God's people were free and clear of the trouble. These aggressive flies would fly in ears and mouths, landing on eyelids and food and everywhere else imaginable.

Like a bad rerun, Pharaoh again promised to let them leave to worship God if only Moses would plead for God to end the plague. Moses did, God did, and Pharaoh hardened up that heart, reposting his "No Exit" sign.

In a change-up from the bugs and critters, the next plague Pharaoh was warned of was one of disease upon the livestock in the fields. God even gave a day's warning, allowing time to bring the creatures in from the field. Like before, the people of Israel, as well as their animals, were spared. The majority of the Egyptians' livestock was not so lucky. Every cow, donkey, camel, and sheep in the fields died. And what happened to Pharaoh's heart? It was hardened. And who did the hardening? Once more, it was Pharaoh, freezing his own heart to the suffering of his own people and the needs of the children of Israel.

Like the third plague, there was no warning before the sixth plague. Boils covered the skin of man and beast. The haughty magicians were struck so bad that they couldn't even stand before Moses and Aaron.

JUST WONDERING: BY THIS POINT, MANY OF THE EGYPTIANS WERE PROBABLY TAKING THE GOD OF ISRAEL SERIOUSLY. WHAT WOULD HAVE HAPPENED IF A CLEVER EGYPTIAN WHO BELIEVED THE WARNING HIRED ONE OF GOD'S PEOPLE TO TAKE HIS LIVESTOCK TO GOSHEN AND WATCH THEM DURING THE DISEASE OUTBREAK?

Puss-oozing sores made it nearly impossible for many of the Egyptians to move. All the same, Pharaoh closed his ears to the words of God. You know the next part. His heart hardened. But this time around, Pharaoh himself did not do the hardening. God did.

God had given Pharaoh chances galore, but it didn't matter. Pharaoh was unwilling to bend, to listen, or to truly repent and take God's lessons to heart. Sadly, this meant that Pharaoh suffered the fate of the perpetually unrepentant; God let him be as unmoved by human care and concern as he wished to be. Mercy cannot be grown in a heart of stone, and those who will not give mercy cannot ever bear to receive it. Pharaoh was locked into his sin. It would take a flood of true repentance to change him, but not a drop of that flowed through his veins.

SEVEN, EIGHT, NINE, NOTHING'S FINE

If the situation for the Egyptians looked bad before, here's where the heat cranked up hellishly. The next announced plague would not be a mere inconvenience or cause of pain. Death, at last, would strike the people of Egypt. Through this, God proclaimed, His name would be known and His power shown to all. Hail beyond any ever seen in that land annihilated everyone and everything in the fields of the Egyptians.

Yet, as bad as the situation was, God showed mercy, instructing the Egyptians to bring the slaves, workers, and animals disease had not killed into their houses. Although Pharaoh's heart was hard, many of his servants now feared the God of Israel and did as He directed. Good thing too, because God sent thunder and hail and fire across the land. That hail was no minor pelting. It was massive and unrelenting, killing every person and animal in the fields, destroying the crops, and damaging every tree. Like with plagues four through seven, the land of Goshen and the people of Israel were spared.

This, at last, freaked Pharaoh out, and he admitted his sin to Moses and Aaron and begged them to ask God to end the hail. This time, he promised to stand by his word and let the people of Israel go. The rest is so predictable that it's sad. Moses did his part, the hail ended, and Pharaoh said, "On second thought, nope."

You'd think Pharaoh would give up. Surely cutting his losses and letting these pesky people of Israel and their destructive God leave would be a relief. But that's not how Pharaoh thought, not even when God threatened a plague of locusts to destroy what few scraps of vegetation still survived. Pharaoh would not be moved even when his own servants pleaded with him,

"Do you not yet understand that Egypt is ruined?" (Exodus 10:7).

For a moment, it looked like he might finally listen. He invited his old enemies, Moses and Aaron, back to the palace and offered to let them go. The longer he talked though, the more annoyed he got, as he tried to set terms and conditions for who and what could leave his land. Pharaoh had no intention of giving them any freedom at all. Thus, the locusts came, devouring everything in their path until "not a green thing remained, neither tree nor plant of the field, through all the land of Egypt" (10:15).

As the cycle continued, with Pharaoh asking Moses to intercede, Moses prayed again on Pharaoh's behalf. How amazing that God gave Moses a heart of compassion, one still willing to pray on his enemy's behalf! Surely, at this point, Moses had little faith that Pharaoh was actually sincere. Nevertheless, he prayed, and the locusts were swept away.

Here is where the story goes dark, literally. Without warning, complete darkness blanketed Egypt. Picture night without any stars, moon, or lights of any sort. There were no flashlights or computer screens to brighten things up. It was so dark that the people had no choice but to stay home for three whole days. The people of Israel, of course, had all the light they needed.

The next part is obvious by now. Pharaoh called for Moses and Aaron, offered to let them go, then backed out of his word. And just to put icing on the cake, Pharaoh threatened to kill them if he ever saw them again. As it turned out, Pharaoh wasn't too far off base. Death was coming soon.

THE FIRSTBORNS DIE

Before Moses left Pharaoh that day, he had one more bit of news to share: at midnight, God would kill every firstborn son in Egypt, including the son of Pharaoh. Even the firstborn cattle would die. Speaking such words, Moses left full of holy anger, and Pharaoh, too, was certainly mad. Yet even this great threat against his people's lives and the life of his own son could not soften Pharaoh's heart. He would not let them go.

Much more could be said about the Passover and the details of preparation God gave to Israel, but let's focus on this point: while the firstborn sons of Egypt would die, the firstborn of Israel would be spared. All it would take was the blood of an unblemished lamb painted on the doorposts and lintels of their houses. God would see this as a sign and pass over their homes as He carried out judgment on the Egyptians.

JUST WONDERING: MOSES KNEW THIS MOMENT WAS COMING BEFORE ANY OF THE PLAGUES BEGAN (EXODUS 4:21–23). WHAT EFFECT DO YOU THINK THIS HAD ON HIM AS THE PLAGUES WERE UNLEASHED? IN MOSES' PLACE, HOW WOULD SUCH KNOWLEDGE HAVE AFFECTED YOU?

How good it is, then, that the people of Israel believed and obeyed Moses when he told them what to do. As a result, they were spared that night, every Israelite house and firstborn son protected by the blood of a lamb.

For the Egyptians, however, the night held only despair as their sons died before their eyes. The anguished cries from every house must have wrenched their broken hearts in two. Pharaoh's own son, his heir, was among the dead, so he called for Moses and Aaron one last time. This time, he demanded that they leave.

At long last, the people of Israel gathered their belongings, along with gold, silver, and clothing—all of this eagerly given by the Egyptians when the Israelites asked for it. These people, who had suffered for their king's hard heart and their own lack of faith in the God of Israel, would do anything to make their former slaves leave and to make the suffering stop.

THAT REMINDS ME: ONCE MORE, JESUS IS CLEARLY IN THE PICTURE. MUCH LIKE THE DARKNESS OF THE NINTH PLAGUE, DARKNESS DESCENDED OVER THE LAND WHILE JESUS WAS ON THE CROSS. IN BOTH INSTANCES, THE DARKNESS IS FOLLOWED BY THE DEATH OF THE FIRSTBORN.

Loaded up, God's people began their journey. No longer slaves, they sought a land of freedom and prosperity.

WHY IS THIS IN THE BIBLE?

This text serves so many purposes that it's impossible to discuss them all in a short space, but here are a few key points:

1. Persistent, arrogant refusal to receive God's Word and direction creates hard hearts that eventually are incapable of hearing and obeying God's voice.

Just like Pharaoh, unbelievers throughout the ages have heard God's Word and refused to heed His commands, believe His warnings, or take advantage of the opportunities He offers for heartfelt repentance. As Moses and Aaron kept going back to Pharaoh, giving him chance after chance to change his ways, we are not to give up on those stuck in the sin of disbelief. Unlike Moses and Aaron, we are not the instruments of judgment; nonetheless, we know the eternal judgment that awaits unbelievers. Speaking clearly of this, we also speak of God's forgiveness and the path He offers to avoid such condemnation.

We cannot tell when a heart has hardened beyond help, so we continue to pray for those stuck in unrepentant sin. Also, we devour God's Word and follow His bidding, eager to never let our hearts become hardened like Pharaoh's.

2. God answered Israel with a resounding yes because they pled to Him for deliverance, and He remembered the promises He had given to their ancestors in the past.

God called Moses to return to Egypt and free His people specifically because they called out for help that only He could give.

3. God always offers deliverance to those who trust in Him.

Countless heroes of the faith in the Bible and beyond have called out to God for deliverance, and He always grants it. He may not save us the way we want to be saved—the Israelites probably weren't thrilled with having to endure some of the plagues—but He will save us. This is especially true when it comes to saving us from sin, death, and the devil.

4. God made certain the people of Israel could never forget the extreme measures He took to free them from slavery and make them His people. In fact, He wants all nations to know and honor His power and authority.

In this crucial part of Scripture, God established His relationship not just with an individual—as He did with Abraham, Isaac, and Jacob (a.k.a. Israel)—but with a large community of people. He and they made promises and commitments to one another. This relationship would carry on through the rest of Scripture and become the forerunner to His relationship with the whole Christian Church. People of all nations and backgrounds can now claim the God who acted so decisively on behalf of Israel.

5. The blood of the Lamb is all that matters when it comes to escaping God's judgment on sin.

The blood of those little lambs smeared on the doors of the people of Israel was nothing special in and of itself. Before and after this event, both believers in God and those who worshiped pagan idols sacrificed animals. What made this blood special is that God commanded its presence and committed Himself to grant mercy to those who trusted in His promise. He turned a matter of life and death into an unquestionable matter of life for those who had faith in Him.

The blood of the Passover lambs saved the people of Israel from an earthly death that for each of them would come around again. The blood of the Lamb of God that has been painted on our hearts is the blood of God Himself. Like at Passover, it has power because God has called us to trust in its ability to save us from judgment. More than that, though, it is the blood of the One who has unending life. Covered with this blood, we have that life too. Covered in it, we do not just escape one little judgment—we are passed straight through the final judgment. Our lives are saved not only for a few earthly years but also for an eternity that we will spend in the presence of this Lamb.

BONUS FEATURES

Favored firstborns: While in modern times most parents are thrilled at the birth of any child, in ancient times the firstborn son wasn't just any child.

- He ensured the continuation of the family line.
- He was trusted to care for his parents in their old age.
- He provided leadership to the rest of the family, including brothers and unmarried sisters.
- He received a greater share of the inheritance. (Twice as much was typical.)
- For the people of Israel, firstborn sons were sacred to God and had to be redeemed by the sacrifice of an animal.

Venerable venery: If you've heard of packs of wolves, flocks of sheep, and schools of fish, you're familiar with terms of venery. Terms of venery are special names given to particular groups of animals. So, when the Egyptians saw the plague pests arriving, knowing the right term to shout in fear could have come in handy.

- An army of frogs
- A horde of gnats
- A swarm of flies
- A plague of locusts (literally, a plague!)

And a few more just for fun:

- An intrusion of cockroaches
- A clowder of cats
- An unkindness of ravens
- A muster of peacocks

CHAPTER 3

SURF'S UP

Who died: The Egyptian army and their horses

How they died: Drowning and the impact of water

Why they died: Arrogance and desire to keep their slaves

When: 1446 BC, not long after the last of the Minoan civilization was destroyed

Where in Scripture: Exodus 13–14

If you needed to defeat an opposing army, what would be at the top of your shopping list? Ranks of trained soldiers? Weapons? Maybe some planes or tanks? How about a general who'd won tons of military victories? By any of these standards, the children of Israel had done a horrible job preparing for their confrontation with Egypt after they left. At least it appeared that way if they looked only at the obvious field general, Moses, and ignored the Lord who commands heaven and earth, the true leader of their community.

That, of course, is exactly what the people of Israel did. This God who'd sent devastating plagues against their enemies and led them out of Egypt should have received the respect He deserved, but Israel seemed to forget all that had just happened.

They were also doing a splendid job of ignoring their heavenly General's ability to improvise (which from His perspective is actually preparation), using anything He wants for any purpose He desires. And with everything in heaven and earth at His disposal, God selected one of the most destructive forces imaginable.

No, not elephants or sharks or rampaging toddlers. Think bigger. Wrecking balls? Too small. Even if you're thinking about natural forces, you're likely focusing on tornadoes, earthquakes, or wildfires. All big and impressively destructive. But they're small-time compared to the power of water.

> **JUST WONDERING:** EXODUS 13:18 SAYS, "THE PEOPLE OF ISRAEL WENT UP OUT OF THE LAND OF EGYPT EQUIPPED FOR BATTLE." HOWEVER, AS FORMER SLAVES THEY HAD NO MILITARY TRAINING, FEW WEAPONS (APART FROM TOOLS), AND NO CHARIOTS, ARMOR, OR OTHER EQUIPMENT. WHY, THEN, DOES THE BIBLE SAY THEY WERE "EQUIPPED FOR BATTLE"?

That is the tool General God used to fight Israel's battle for them. And there was no weapon better suited to the task.

But before we get to main event, let's take a few steps back and join in the march from Egypt.

PILLAR PARADE

When the people of Israel left Pharaoh's control and their old home in Goshen, they traveled a number of miles to a place called Succoth. There, they paused briefly to catch their breath and receive instructions from the Lord about future Passover celebrations and the consecration of the first-born. There was no time to wait around, though, because they still weren't far from Pharaoh and their hated lives of slavery—that they had paradoxically been rather comfortable in.

God was quite aware of this as He planned the next part of their route. Rather than guiding them on the shortcut through the land of the Philistines, God led them through the wilderness toward the Red Sea. He knew that although the people wanted freedom, their resolve to make this journey to Canaan was weak, and seeing war among the Philistines might have been too much for their incomplete faith in God's ability to keep them alive during their journey. God wasn't about to let them retreat to the familiarity of Egypt at the first sign of trouble. He hadn't freed them for nothing. He was taking them to a place where they would have no choice but to trust Him and commit to their future path.

There's one aspect of all this that most people find hard to grasp. There weren't just 1,000 or 10,000 or even 50,000 Israelites marching through the wilderness. The Bible says there were 600,000 men over the age of 20, meaning that counting women and children too, there were 2,000,000 or more Israelites making this journey! That's the size of a large modern city. It's not the kind of group Moses could just shout to, expecting everyone to hear. Imagine a crowd of people stretching out as far as the eye could see. Even traveling in a wide swath, the line would've stretched for miles. And with whole families in tow, they didn't exactly move fast.

THAT REMINDS ME: IN GENESIS 50:24–25, AN OLD AND DYING JOSEPH INSISTED THAT THE CHILDREN OF ISRAEL WOULD ONE DAY RETURN TO CANAAN. HE MADE HIS FAMILY SWEAR THAT WHEN THAT HAPPENED, THEY WOULD TAKE HIS BONES ALONG AND BURY THEM IN THE PROMISED LAND. MOSES HONORED THIS REQUEST, BRINGING JOSEPH'S SKELETON ALONG FOR THE JOURNEY.

God refused to provide the Israelites with excuses or allow them to forget that He was with them, so, as they walked, God Himself led them in a pillar of cloud by day and a pillar of fire by night. With such visible signs, God's presence was clear, and there was no chance of people at the back of the crowd losing their way or wandering off the chosen path. Traveling by day and night put them further and further away from their old lives and Pharaoh, both important accomplishments.

At last they came to the Red Sea, or sea of reeds, and God commanded them to stop and make camp. By this point, they'd traveled a fair distance, far enough for Pharaoh to be sure they weren't coming back. Yet God knew how that arrogant king thought. He knew that Pharaoh would mistake their wandering path for an error and that he would pursue them. God was more than ready for this opportunity to teach the Egyptians once and for all who was superior.

As always, God was right. Pharaoh was filled once more with desire to rule over the people of Israel and force them back to Egypt. He personally led the charge of six hundred elite chariots, all the regular chariots, and his army of trained soldiers. When they caught up with Israel, it's no wonder the Israelites were terrified. They saw themselves as ill-equipped, untrained, and clustered together with old folks and women and children. Pharaoh's army appeared unstoppable.

Then again, they'd forgotten which side the Unstoppable One was on.

THE KING OF THE CROSSING GUARDS

As the mighty Egyptian army closed in, the Israelites engaged in what would soon become their favorite activity: whining. To Moses they said, "Is it because there are no graves in Egypt that you have taken us away to die in the wilderness?" (Exodus 14:11) They went on to complain that they never wanted to leave Egypt. Basically, they accused Moses of forcing them all to leave slavery against their will.

Remember again that there were millions of Israelites and one Moses. He couldn't really force them to do anything. Moreover, only once before had they objected to Moses' actions on their behalf. The rest of the time, they'd happily agreed to God's plan communicated by Moses and Aaron. Their memories were more full of holes than old socks because they'd also forgotten God's glorious demonstrations of power over the Egyptians through the plagues.

THAT REMINDS ME: ALTHOUGH THE ISRAELITES AT THIS POINT SHOWED A WEAKER FAITH THAN THEY SHOULD HAVE, THEIR FAITH WAS CELEBRATED FAR BEYOND THAT DAY NONETHELESS. VERSE 29 OF THE GREAT HEROES OF THE FAITH CHAPTER, HEBREWS 11, SAYS, "BY FAITH THE PEOPLE CROSSED THE RED SEA AS ON DRY LAND, BUT THE EGYPTIANS, WHEN THEY ATTEMPTED TO DO THE SAME, WERE DROWNED."

To Moses' credit, he didn't chew them out for their lack of faith. Instead, he gave a pep talk: "Don't be afraid. God will save you, so shut up, and watch the Lord fight for you."

God backed up Moses' words big time with a promise of His own to let the Israelites cross through the sea on dry land. And just to keep Pharaoh's forces away from the Israelites, the angel of God stood behind the children of Israel, along with the pillar of cloud and fire. So the Israelites had light, while the Egyptians were left in darkness.

The big moment had arrived, and you can just imagine the shock and awe on the faces of the Israelites as Moses stretched out his hand over the sea and an insanely powerful wind forced the water back on both sides, creating a path right down the middle. The Red Sea was not some little creek or ten-foot wide trickle of a river that had dried up before they got there. This was a massive body of water, impossible to cross on foot until the Lord drove the sea back. And it's not like this was a simple sandbar at low tide. The Bible explicitly says there were two walls of water, one on the Israelites' right side and one on their left. Have you ever passed through a corridor like that?

Many zoos and aquariums have underwater tunnels where visitors can watch fish, seals, and other sea creatures swim next to them—and sometimes above them—held back only by see-through walls. Imagine walking through one of those, only without the glass or plastic walls to hold back the water. Imagine seeing the water stand up on its own, held in place only by the wind and the power of God. It would be breathtaking and terrifying.

Even for those Israelites who'd paid attention during the plagues, this was something special. It wasn't a miracle they could explain away or view from a distance. They were right in the middle of it. And it was massive, mighty, and all for them. God did it for them.

One of the most amazing miracles that the Israelites discovered as Moses herded them into this water-walled corridor was that the ground was dry. It should have been mucky and muddy, causing their feet to slip and to sink into the ground. But this was no natural phenomenon. It was the hand of God, and He can do whatever He wants to help the people He calls His own.

Once these two million or so Israelites had a significant head start through the divided sea—again, this wasn't just twenty or thirty feet they were crossing—God's angel and the pillar moved aside and let the Egyptians follow, which the Egyptian army did eagerly. All of Pharaoh's chariots and horses rushed toward the runaway Israelites. The Egyptians thought they had a sure thing. An ill-prepared, slow-moving group of slaves against their spears and swords and killer chariots. Better yet, morning was coming, meaning they'd have a clear line of sight for the kill. All they had to do was get to the Israelites, who had just exited the path onto the other shore, and the whole thing would be over.

That's when God whipped out a big old can of "not so fast." From the pillar of cloud and fire, God "threw the Egyptian forces into a panic, clogging their chariot wheels so that they drove heavily" (14:24–25). Suddenly, this dry ground turned back into mud and wet sand. Instant panic. "Run for it!" the Egyptians yelled as they tried to turn around. "The Lord fights for them, not us!" The army knew they were beaten.

But Egypt had pushed it too far, and God was not ready to let them go. Crossing guard Moses reached out his hand at God's command, and those high walls of water crashed down on the Egyptian army. Every horse, every chariot, every soldier was smacked down by two mighty waves.

JUST WONDERING: THIS ACCOUNT REFERS BOTH TO THE LORD AND TO THE ANGEL OF GOD IN ASSOCIATION WITH THE PILLAR OF CLOUD AND FIRE. WHO IS THIS ANGEL? CAN YOU THINK OF OTHER TIMES "THE ANGEL OF THE LORD" APPEARS IN THE OLD TESTAMENT?

Many were crushed to death by the brutal impact of the water—for that much water is extremely heavy—and smashed to death by collisions of horses and chariots and bodies. The rest drowned, their lungs sputtering to inhale, unable to get the tiniest breath. Think of a time you started choking badly or saw it happen to someone else. That's a scary moment. Now add water to that, so that even if the choking stops, there's no new air to come in. What a horrible last few seconds that would be.

> **JUST WONDERING:** WHILE WE'RE TOLD THAT ALL THE CHARIOTS, HORSES, AND HORSEMEN PERISHED, IT'S POSSIBLE THAT SOME FOOT-SOLDIERS, COMMANDERS, AND PERHAPS PHARAOH HIMSELF REMAINED ON THE OPPOSITE BANK. HOW MIGHT THIS EVENT HAVE AFFECTED THE REST OF THEIR LIVES? HOW MIGHT THEY HAVE DESCRIBED IT TO OTHERS?

As the sea closed on top of the Egyptians and the path to Egypt with it, two facts were crystal clear to the people of Israel, these millions of homeless refugees. First, their God was to be trusted and feared. Second, there was no going back.

WHY IS THIS IN THE BIBLE?

This touchstone event was the irrefutable conclusion to God's deliverance of the Israelites from their slavery in Egypt. It changed everything. For the first time in more than four hundred years, no one ruled over them and they had no idea what the next day would bring. The book on their slavery was closed, and now, like their ancestor Abraham, they were being led by God to a new land, where they were promised prosperity and a home.

Another miracle of sorts happened as the Israelites stared at the water behind them: they believed in the Lord and in Moses. They, at last, expressed universal trust in the God who'd been working for their good all along. What's more, they feared Him. He was on their side, and after seeing what He could do, they had no desire to ever be His enemy. This fear, trust, and love for God faded at times, but from this day forward, the Red Sea would always be a stark reminder of who was in charge.

JUST WONDERING: MODERN SCHOLARS OFTEN OBSESS ABOUT FINDING NON-SUPERNATURAL CAUSES FOR MAJOR BIBLICAL MIRACLES. WHILE GOD CERTAINLY USES NATURE TO PERFORM MANY OF HIS GREAT DEEDS FOR US, WHY IS IT DANGEROUS TO TRY TO EXPLAIN AWAY MIRACLES SOLELY WITH SCIENCE? ON THE OTHER HAND, IN WHAT WAYS CAN SCIENCE BE AN AID TO CHRISTIANS IN EXPLAINING THEIR FAITH?

For us, this miracle, like all miracles in the Old Testament, shows that God has the desire and the power to take care of His people no matter what forces stand in opposition. Just as the people of Israel knew that this miracle was for them, we know that as God's New Testament people of faith, this miracle is also for us. Through the sea crossing, He preserved the ancestors of Jesus and the people of faith who called on God's name.

What's more, their passage through the Red Sea is often mentioned as an image of what happens for us in Baptism (see 1 Corinthians 10:1–4). We pass through the waters of Baptism to leave behind our former roles as slaves to sin. Much like Pharaoh's army, our old sinful natures are drowned in Baptism's water, and we are led safely through, a fact in which we rejoice. From there, we, like the Israelites, set forth on the journey of our lives, trusting God and longing for the day when we will enter the true promised land of heaven.

BONUS FEATURES

Beating the odds: Pharaoh's army is not the only example of a seemingly stronger force being taken down a by a "lesser" opponent. Here are a couple more from the pages of history.

The Assyrian army outside Jerusalem: During the reign of King Hezekiah of Judah, the Assyrian army appeared unstoppable. They'd successfully besieged Samaria, defeated Israel, and taken the people away to Assyria as captives, and had recently laid the smack down on the fortified cities of Judah. Hezekiah was so scared that he stripped the silver and gold from the treasury and from the walls and doors of the temple itself and sent that as a peace offering to the king of Assyria. That failed miserably, and soon a massive Assyrian army waited outside Jerusalem, Judah's capital, to destroy the city and take them away as well. Then the unexpected happened. Hezekiah prayed and Isaiah prophesied. That night, the angel of the Lord swept down and killed 185,000 Assyrian soldiers before dawn. Needless to say, the Assyrians left Judah alone for a while. (For more about this battle, see 2 Chronicles 32; 2 Kings 18; or Isaiah 36–39.)

Morgarten: Duke Leopold I of Austria, the leader of an invading group of soldiers and cavalry (soldiers on horses), had equipped his soldiers well with heavy chain mail and armor. Even the horses were armored. His intent was to ride through the mountains of Switzerland smashing heads and scaring peasants until they surrendered. That seemed a great plan until, on November 15, 1315, a force of 1,500 Swiss Confederates ambushed the much larger force by blocking the road at a spot where one side was a steep slope and the other a swamp. The unarmored Swiss, who had positioned themselves above on the hillside, rained down boulders, logs, and halberds (part axe, part spear, part hook). Most of the invaders who weren't killed were forced off the road and into the swamp.

For more stories of big victories against superior forces, check out the Battle of Marathon, the Battle of Isandlwana, and the Battle of the Golan Heights on the Internet or at a library near you.

Song and dance: Immediately following God's deliverance of them through the Red Sea, Moses and the people of Israel were filled with so much joy that they sang a rousing song of God's victory for them. Moses' sister Miriam and the women followed up with tambourines, dancing, and more song: "Sing to the LORD, for He has triumphed gloriously; the horse and his rider He has thrown into the sea" (Exodus 15:21).

The Bible records a number of other times when God's people worshiped Him through song (even if spoken) or dance. Read these passages to learn more:

- *2 Samuel 6:14*: David danced before the ark of the covenant as it was brought into Jerusalem.
- *The Psalms*: The Bible's song and prayer book is packed with praise and pleas for help.
- *Luke 1:46–55*: In what we call the Magnificat, Mary sang about God's great blessing to her through the child in her womb.
- *Revelation 15:2–4*: The saints are continually singing praise to God, as they do in these verses in the Book of Revelation.

CHAPTER 4

DYING FOR A BITE

Who died: Many of the people of Israel

How they died: Snakebites

Why they died: Whining and complaining

When: 1407 BC, roughly the same time as the composition of the oldest surviving written melody, Hurrian Hymn Text H6

Where in Scripture: Numbers 21:4–9

Who's the whiniest person you know? Can you imagine his or her worst, most irritating whine? Can you hear the screechy voice and absurd reasons for complaining? Okay. Now take that one person and add thousands more just as bad; then imagine the whining going on and on and on for months, years, decades. That's what Moses and God had to put up with.

The children of Israel were already whiny when they reached the Red Sea. It didn't get better from there. It's hard to imagine any parent having to deal with as much complaining as the people of Israel leveled at Moses and God. They complained about everything!

They complained about bread and meat. They complained about water. They complained that Moses was taking too long receiving the Ten Commandments. They complained about getting the wrong food and missing vegetables. They complained about Moses and Aaron being in charge. They complained about water again. And finally they complained about God, Moses, food, water, and the likelihood that they would all die in the desert.

Over and over, God answered their whining. He gave them bread from heaven, meat, and water from a rock, but every so often, they simply pushed it too far. It was time to lock down on their sinful grumblings and point them back toward the path of trust and obedience. And with these people, giving them what they asked for simply didn't do the trick. They needed a serious wakeup call.

ENTER THE SNAKES

It should have been enough for Moses to say, "Hey, guys, God's brought us this far. Stick with the program." Maybe a nice reminder of the plagues God used to pry their families free from Egypt and His miraculous opening of the Red Sea would do the trick. Not to mention decades of food, water, protection, and leadership while they were wandering in the wilderness. But, no, the children of Israel were slow to get it. Yet again they cried to Moses, "Why have you and God brought us out here to die? And, by the way, that food God gives us so we won't starve really stinks. How about something better?"

JUST WONDERING: THE WILDERNESS WANDERINGS ESTABLISH THE OLD TESTAMENT THEME OF PEOPLE COMPLAINING AND DISOBEYING AND GOD PUNISHING AND THEN SAVING. WHY IS IT EASIER TO BLAME GOD WHEN THINGS GO BAD THAN TO GIVE HIM CREDIT WHEN THINGS GO WELL?

This generation of Israelites really had no excuse for their wrong focus. These weren't the original adults who'd left Egypt nearly forty years earlier. Those Israelites had stood on the borders on Canaan, rejected the reports of Joshua and Caleb, and begged to go back to Egypt. God was so fed up with them, He was ready to strike them down and create a new nation from Moses (Numbers 14). Instead, Moses intervened on the people's behalf, and God spared them. However, no one older than twenty years at that point would live to enter the Promised Land. Instead, they would spend the next forty years wandering the wilderness until the adults all died off.

The complainers at this point, then, were the children and grandchildren

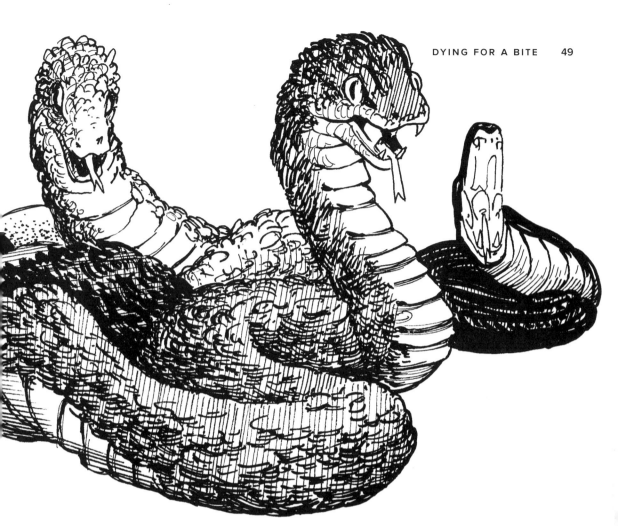

of the original Israelite adults. Most or all of their lives had been spent in the wilderness with Moses leading them and God ruling over and providing for them. They'd had ample time to see God's continued care and miraculous protection and to hear the stories of God's might from their parents. Instead, they inherited their parents' skewed memories and grumbling nature. And they let loose the complaints full force against tired, old Moses and their ever-faithful God.

And then came "sssssssssssssssnakes." Everywhere among the millions of traveling, complaining people, snakes sneaked their way in. In the Israelites' tents, by their fires, in the dust before them,

JUST WONDERING: THE REGION THEY'D LIVED IN FOR THE PAST FORTY YEARS HAD MORE THAN ITS SHARE OF SNAKES AND SCORPIONS, BUT THIS IS THE ONLY ENCOUNTER THE BIBLE MENTIONS. IS IT LIKELY THAT THE ISRAELITES EVER THOUGHT TO THANK GOD FOR PROTECTING THEM ALL THOSE OTHER TIMES? WHAT DANGERS IN THE WORLD AROUND YOU DOES GOD PROTECT YOU FROM WITHOUT YOUR THANKS OR AWARENESS?

the hissers could not be avoided. But after all their ridiculous complaining, the snakes, or something like that, should have been no surprise.

And these weren't just any snakes. Fiery serpents slithered between the people's feet, biting and killing. While "fiery" may have referred to their shiny, metallic-like skin, it likely also applied to the intense pain of their poisonous bites. Most snakebites are not lethal, but those that are can kill in a variety of horrible ways. They can result in a burning sensation that runs through the body, and the poison can eat away at the flesh. They can destroy brain cells, disrupting the nervous system and paralyzing muscles. Some snake venom will prevent blood from clotting, making it easier to bleed out, and some makes the blood coagulate, becoming so thick and goopy it can't flow properly. Inflammation, chills, and breathing difficulties are just some of the laundry list of symptoms snake venom can bring. In the end, death can come quickly or take days.

With these particular snakes, we know only that their bite was painful, lethal, and that death took at least a little while to come. The Israelites were in a world of hurt, as the snakes bit everyone in their paths and people died all around. Then something important happened. For the first time in a good while, they realized it was all their fault. Theirs. Not Moses' fault. Not God's fault. Their fault.

THAT REMINDS ME: JOHN 3:14–15 SAYS, "AS MOSES LIFTED UP THE SERPENT IN THE WILDERNESS, SO MUST THE SON OF MAN BE LIFTED UP, THAT WHOEVER BELIEVES IN HIM MAY HAVE ETERNAL LIFE."

Amazingly, they did exactly the right thing for once. They came to God's representative, Moses, and admitted what boneheads they'd been. They confessed their sin for saying stupid stuff against Moses and God and begged their human leader to pray to God on their behalf. Given how whiny and disobedient they'd been, they must have figured God would not want to hear from them directly. It's a testament to his character that Moses was willing to intercede, especially since this incident came shortly after the death of his beloved brother, Aaron. But Moses prayed to God, and God answered.

If God was like us, He might have made them sweat longer, or He might have at least answered back with a sarcastic, "Really? You don't like My snakes either?" A perverse god might have replaced their daily manna and quail with snake meat just to rub it in. But our God isn't like that.

Immediately, He told Moses to forge a bronze serpent and put in on a pole for anyone snakebitten to look at. Instead of dying, that person would live. Something that looked like death would give life. Of course, the bronze snake wasn't the one saving them. It was no idol, no object of worship. They were delivered from death because they trusted God's power to heal them and obeyed His command. God alone deserves to be worshiped.

Keep in mind that God didn't let them completely off the hook. He didn't make the snakes disappear. They were still there, and they were still biting people. Sin has consequences. It causes suffering. For them and for us. But with God's mercy, sin does not have to cause death.

> THAT REMINDS ME: ALMOST SEVEN HUNDRED YEARS LATER, KING HEZEKIAH DESTROYED THE BRONZE SERPENT BECAUSE THE PEOPLE OF ISRAEL WERE WORSHIPING IT (2 KINGS 18:4).

WHY IS THIS IN THE BIBLE?

Of all the failures of human beings, complaining may be the least condemned and the most performed. We all complain, from the holiest pastor to the most privileged billionaire. No one has everything he or she wants all the time, and everyone has at least one or two favorite people to vent complaints to. Have you ever tried not to complain for a week? It's nearly impossible.

Like the Israelites of old, we complain about how God doesn't give us all we want. We show a lack of trust in Him. In short, we sin. And our sin, too, causes suffering, much of it self-inflicted, but God does not desire that to result in our eternal death. Instead, He sent something that looked like death to give life. He sent His Son to die on the cross to give us new and eternal life in heaven. Not the death we deserved. Not even eternal suffering.

The Early Church Fathers, the pastors and teachers of the faith in the centuries after Jesus' earthly ministry, taught that the stick the snake was put on was in the shape of the cross. In Christ, that serpent—the symbol of the devil—was replaced with the man who was God. What a brilliant image for then and for now! The snake they looked at gave short-term deliverance, but looking at Jesus with eyes of faith gives life that cannot and will not end.

This account shows us our sinful natures, the consequences of sin, and God's ever-patient willingness to help us in all our problems. He asks only that we look to and trust Him for deliverance.

BONUS FEATURES

Killer critters: In our time, people still die of snakebites, but not usually. Even deadly bites can be treated with antivenoms and other medical interventions. Still, there are plenty of other creatures that can put a kink in your plans to live to a ripe old age.

Stonefish: Camouflaged on the seabed in tropical waters, the stonefish bears thirteen needlelike spines filled with neurotoxin. Its sting is said to be so painful that people have begged for the affected limb to be amputated.

Inland taipan: Although responsible for few deaths because it lives in Australian deserts, the inland taipan packs enough venom in one bite to kill one hundred men.

Brazilian wandering spider: The deadliest spider in the world, 0.006 mg of its venom can kill a mouse. It's responsible for many deaths largely because it enjoys highly populated areas.

Australian box jellyfish: Responsible for thousands of deaths, its insanely powerful venom can be delivered through thousands of stinging cells. Without immediate treatment, death is nearly certain as the heart fails, shock sets in, or the victim drowns.

Blue-ringed octopus: The golf-ball size octopus packs a mean wallop.

Its venom is one thousand times stronger than cyanide, paralyzes its victims, and leaves them unable to breathe.

Mosquitoes: Although the average mosquito is merely a nuisance—a bite resulting in an unwanted itch that lasts a few days— these bugs transmit diseases to hundreds of millions of people a year, resulting in millions of deaths.

Unclean! Unclean! Snakes are just one of many animals that Leviticus identified as improper or unclean for the people of Israel to eat. While the New Testament lifted these restrictions, here are some of the other unclean animals Leviticus listed:

- Camels
- Rabbits
- Lobsters
- Ostriches
- Mole rats
- Lizards
- Rock badgers
- Pigs
- Eagles
- Snails
- Oysters

CHAPTER 5

Getting a Bellyful

Who died: Eglon / 10,000 Moabite soldiers

How they died: Sword in the stomach / battle

Why they died: Oppression of God's people, greed, lack of caution

When: Circa 1314 BC, around the time that Enlil-nirari succeeded his father as king of Assyria

Where in Scripture: Judges 3:12–30

Stupid, fat king gets stabbed. Bathroom jokes abound. The end. It's tempting to summarize the story of Eglon that way. We don't know much about the king, and his death seems like a straightforward Sunday School lecture about keeping in shape, not being gullible, and not opposing the children of Israel. There is, as always, more to it than that.

It starts with understanding that as much as Eglon's death is a weighty matter, the story isn't really all about him. Rather, consider this to be a continuation of the snakebite story from Exodus. It's the tale of tiny sins that grow too big to ignore. Pun intended.

THE PERILOUS PATTERN

One of the problems with sin is that, over time, even "small" sins escalate into monstrous messes. Following their time wandering in the desert with Moses and their conquering the Promised Land with Joshua, the people of Israel one-upped their earlier complaints with straight-out acts of evil. "They turned back and were more corrupt than their fathers, going after other gods, serving them and bowing down to them. They did not drop any of their practices or their stubborn ways" (Judges 2:19). Eventually, they would repent, God would send a judge to save them, and they'd have peace for a while. Then they would fall back into idolatry and other sins. This became the pattern during the time of the judges and, later, the kings.

Here's the simple version:

1. God saves His people or empowers someone to save them.
2. Time passes, and they forget about God and do evil.
3. God sends an enemy kingdom to punish and remind them.
4. They "remember" God and pray to Him to save them.

Repeat steps 1–4 over and over and over.

It's not like they had any excuse at this point. Their families had seen more miracles and mighty acts of God than anyone in history. Yet somehow over the course of a generation or two, the tales of God's wondrous protection apparently weren't stressed all that much to the Israelites' kids and grandkids. Obviously, there's a big difference between something that happened to your mom or your grandfather and something that happens to you.

JUST WONDERING: MOST EVENTS THAT SEEMED SIGNIFICANT IN YOUR GRANDPARENTS' LIFETIME PROBABLY SEEM LESS IMPORTANT TO YOU. HOW IS THIS TYPE OF PERCEPTION A CHALLENGE FOR PEOPLE WHO HAVE HEARD OF JESUS BUT DIDN'T WITNESS HIS DEATH OR RESURRECTION? IN WHAT WAYS CAN THIS DISTANCE BETWEEN US AND JESUS' LIFE ON EARTH BE OVERCOME?

Obviously, you'll feel more strongly about one than the other. Still, you'd think that parents and grandparents who'd seen the plagues, the parting of the Red Sea, the miracle manna, the bronze serpent, and the sun itself stand still in the sky would make sure God's greatness was clearly communicated to following generations.

But did they? Not so much. The people of the Lord fell away and fell away and fell away again from living as God commanded. This was the situation when King Eglon of Moab took charge. God's people had done evil again, so God sent Eglon in to conquer the people of Israel. A pretty direct reminder to turn away from evil, right?

In response, they prayed to God for help right away. Not! Not a day later, not a month later, not even a year later was there any sign of repentance. The years passed. Two, three, four. Finally, eight years later, the people of Israel woke themselves from their idiocy and cried out to God for help.

THAT REMINDS ME: THERE'S NO REASON TO WAIT TO ASK FOR GOD'S DELIVERANCE. HE TELLS US, "CALL UPON ME IN THE DAY OF TROUBLE; I WILL DELIVER YOU, AND YOU SHALL GLORIFY ME" (PSALM 50:15).

And though their cries for help were slow in coming, God's reply was not. He strengthened a man named Ehud to deliver His people.

HERE COMES THE JUDGE

In our day, a judge is someone stern in a black robe who sits in an orderly courtroom. Often they're selected for their academic prowess, lawyerly experience, and political connections. It's not their job to catch criminals or carry out the actual punishments. They merely deliver decisions for others to act on.

There was no dress code for judges in Old Testament times, and their selection had little to do with their backgrounds. God picked whomever He saw fit to help His people. These judges fit the old cliché of "judge, jury, and executioner" just right, especially if you add "cop" to that because they often had to catch the guilty first. By and large, being a judge in those days meant being a man of action, a champion who was not afraid of leaving a trail of blood in his wake.

History makes it clear that the judges were far from perfect. That's okay. It wasn't their job to model perfection. Their job was to carry out the will of the Perfect One by saving His chosen people from their enemies.

EGLON AND EHUD

Aided by his allies, the Ammonites and the Amalekites, King Eglon of Moab had conquered the repopulated Jericho and all Israel. Sitting in his palace, growing fat on the abundance of Israel for eighteen years, Eglon was content to let the wealth keep rolling in—for eighteen years. One of the best things about being a conqueror was collecting regular tribute—think mega taxes—from the people who were conquered.

As this tale starts, the time had come for another great big tribute payment from Israel to Eglon, and wouldn't you know it, Israel found just the guy to deliver the wealth. A man named Ehud, a Benjaminite whom God had chosen to be their judge and deliverer. Who better to deliver than a deliverer?

THAT REMINDS ME: ANOTHER PROMINENT PLACE THE BIBLE SPEAKS OF MOAB IS IN THE BOOK OF RUTH. RUTH IS A MOABITE, AND MOAB IS WHERE HER FATHER-IN-LAW AND MOTHER-IN-LAW, NAOMI, MOVED WITH THEIR THREE SONS TO AVOID FAMINE. ALTHOUGH A FOREIGNER, RUTH BECAME ONE OF GOD'S PEOPLE AND AN ANCESTOR OF KING DAVID. RUTH ALSO LIVED DURING THE TIME OF THE JUDGES.

Oh, and one more critical fact about Ehud: he was left-handed. The text literally says his right hand was restricted, meaning his hand may have been crippled or wounded in some way.

Anyway, left-handed Ehud and the people carrying the tribute—it would have been heavy!—set out to deliver the good stuff to the king. Also, knowing that delivering the tribute wouldn't be enough to help his people, Ehud had strapped a sword to his right thigh and hidden it under his clothes. Tricky guy, that Ehud. Since most people would strap a sword to the left side to make it easy to draw across the body, the Moabite guards wouldn't be inclined to check Ehud's right side for a weapon. Beyond that, someone with a restricted hand, like Ehud, wouldn't look like much of a threat.

Next thing you know, Ehud and the tribute carriers were before King Eglon presenting the tribute. If Ehud used that sword right then, he'd have a perfect shot at the king, who was likely distracted by his new pile of gold and silver. But that wasn't Ehud's style. Instead, he walked away with the now empty-handed tribute handlers before turning around again for another visit with Eglon.

What took place next is one of history's bazillion examples of a simple truth: people

> **THAT REMINDS ME:** PROVERBS 26:22 PROVIDES INSIGHT INTO THE LINGERING EFFECTS OF SECRETS: "THE WORDS OF A WHISPERER ARE LIKE DELICIOUS MORSELS; THEY GO DOWN INTO THE INNER PARTS OF THE BODY."

love secrets. Whether they are secrets about themselves, about someone else, or just plain old dirty gossip about the old woman with the goose in the village, secrets are like magnets for greedy minds. And did Eglon have a greedy mind? You betcha.

So, when Ehud said, "I have a secret message for you, O king" (Judges 3:19), Eglon couldn't get rid of his royal attendants fast enough. He sent them from the room so he and Ehud could share the juicy news in private. After all, Ehud didn't look like a mighty warrior, and he'd just brought the tribute personally. If you can't trust a guy who brings you treasure, who can you trust?

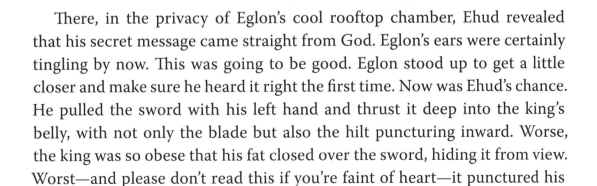

There, in the privacy of Eglon's cool rooftop chamber, Ehud revealed that his secret message came straight from God. Eglon's ears were certainly tingling by now. This was going to be good. Eglon stood up to get a little closer and make sure he heard it right the first time. Now was Ehud's chance. He pulled the sword with his left hand and thrust it deep into the king's belly, with not only the blade but also the hilt puncturing inward. Worse, the king was so obese that his fat closed over the sword, hiding it from view. Worst—and please don't read this if you're faint of heart—it punctured his bowels so that poop plopped out.

Ehud closed the doors to the roof chamber, locked them, and made a beeline out of there. Eglon remained dead and disgusting alone.

The servants went up and noticed the locked doors but didn't go in. This was their king, after all, and disturbing a king who wanted privacy was a good way to get yourself killed. Plus, they probably smelled something, which led them to their next bad conclusion that he was just using the bathroom. Thus, they waited and waited until they were so embarrassed and concerned that they unlocked the chamber and went in. The king was not on the toilet after all.

JUST WONDERING: WHAT DO YOU THINK EGLON'S SERVANTS DID NEXT? DID THEY BLAME ONE ANOTHER, FOCUS ON CATCHING THE ASSASSIN, OR PREPARE FOR A ROYAL FUNERAL? HOW WOULD THEY EVEN BEGIN TO EXPLAIN WHAT HAD HAPPENED TO THE NEXT KING OF MOAB?

Their delay was good news for Ehud because it gave him plenty of time to escape. Not only that, but he sounded the trumpets, calling many of the people of Israel to him. When he said, "Follow after me, for the LORD has given your enemies the Moabites into your hand" (3:28), a good crowd followed him. They intercepted the now leaderless Moabite troops at the ford and killed ten thousand soldiers—not one man escaped. And that was the end of Moabite rule in Israel.

God also had one more gift to give. From that time on, there was peace in the land for eighty years, as long as Ehud lived.

WHY IS THIS IN THE BIBLE?

Do you remember that pattern from earlier?

1. God saves His people or empowers someone to save them.
2. Time passes, and they forget about God and do evil.
3. God sends an enemy kingdom to punish and remind them.
4. They "remember" God and pray to Him to save them.

Repeat.

The pattern of our lives as Christians is similar.

1. God saved us, once and for all, by sending His Son as our deliverer from sin, death, and hell.
2. Time passes, and we lose our focus on what God has done for us. Despite being His people, we sin.
3. Our sins themselves bring punishment, in the form of moving us away from God's will, which moves us away from His gifts.
4. We remember what God has already done for us and pray to Him for forgiveness.

While the similarities are obvious, note the key differences too.

1. God no longer sends multiple judges or deliverers for multiple acts of deliverance. One deliverer, Jesus Christ, is all it takes to save us from our countless acts of rebellion.
2. For those who hold firmly to faith in Christ, sin still comes, and we do what is evil; however, by His grace we do not wholly abandon His will and His ways.
3. God does not send enemies upon us. We bring them upon ourselves by choosing to sin and avoiding God's forgiveness.

Certainly, we could also take from this account lessons about pride and gluttony. It is better, however, to focus on how fortunate we are to have God as our protector. He will never cease to deliver from evil those who call on His name and receive His good gifts. God does not want us to ever continue in our suffering. Rather, He longs for us to respond to suffering with increased dependence on and trust in His gracious and merciful will to act for our benefit.

BONUS FEATURES

Handing it to lefties: Historically, many sayings about the left hand are not exactly compliments. Our modern word *sinister*, meaning "evil," originally was a reference to the left hand. Left-handed (or underhanded) compliments are insults disguised as compliments. For example, saying, "You've never looked more beautiful" to a woman wearing a sack over her head is a left-handed compliment.

In certain cultures and eras, being a lefty was considered a mark of weakness or of an inclination toward evil. In reality, many lefties have stood strong for their beliefs, and being a lefty can have advantages.

In ancient times, warriors were used to fighting mostly right-handed opponents. This meant that facing a lefty could be unpredictable, since the lefty moved the opposite way of what his opponent's fighting habits said. Many lefties have excelled in sports such as tennis, boxing, and baseball precisely because their angles of attack tend to be different than the typical right-handed opponents most athletes prepare for.

While the right hand is mentioned in the Bible more often in regard to the highest position and the most generosity and power, at other times it is made clear that the left hand is also a place of blessings, as in Proverbs 3:16; Song of Solomon 2:6; and Mark 10:37–40.

Famous lefties: Since they make up roughly 10–12 percent of the population, you know there's a lot of them out there. Here's just a sampling of some of the most famous purported and proven lefties:

Presidents: Obama, Clinton, George H. W. Bush, Truman

Artists and Authors: M. C. Escher, Michelangelo, Albrecht Dürer, H. G. Wells, Lewis Carroll

Actors: Charlie Chaplin, George Burns, W. C. Fields, Jerry Seinfeld, Oprah Winfrey

Athletes: Oscar de la Hoya, Gayle Sayers, Larry Bird, Shoeless Joe Jackson

Leaders: Alexander the Great, Julius Caesar, Fidel Castro, England's Prince William

CHAPTER 6

Staking a Claim

Who died: Sisera / his army

How they died: Tent stake in the head / swords

Why they died: Cruelty and oppression

When: Circa 1217 BC, around the time that the Olmec civilization began flourishing in what is now the southern part of Mexico

Where in Scripture: Judges 4–5

One woman personally accompanies a general to make him go into battle, while another brutally kills the opposing general. The day is won, the enemy defeated, and peace is earned for forty years, all by the actions of two women. And your response is probably along the lines of "Yeah, so what?"

That would not always have been the case. This account is not as shocking to us now as it was to people years ago. We live in an age when women are no longer assumed to be damsels in distress. That, however, was not the culture at the time of Deborah.

Keeping in mind that the Bible is no mere book of stories but a book of true history, let's try an exercise. Make a list of men in the Bible who could be the hero or co-hero in an action movie. No sweat, right? Abraham, Joseph, Moses, Noah, David, Samson, Joshua, Elijah, Elisha, Daniel. Another dozen Old Testament judges, kings, and prophets could easily make the cut. Even Paul and Jesus probably qualify.

Now make a similar list of action heroines for women. It's not so easy. This story gives two: Deborah and Jael. Depending on how you define action movies, maybe Esther and Miriam could be added to the list.

None of this is to say that the Bible is not a book about women. It is. And the roles they play are hugely important. But by and large, they are celebrated as faithful daughters, mothers, wives, and followers. Perfect for leads or co-leads in a romance, Oscar-nominated drama, or inspirational movie, but action was simply not the prime domain of woman in Bible times. It went against the grain of the male-dominated cultures.

JUST WONDERING: HOW DO YOU THINK THE AVERAGE MALE OF OLD TESTAMENT TIMES WOULD HAVE RESPONDED IF TOLD THAT TWO WOMEN WOULD SAVE HIM AND HIS PEOPLE FROM AN ENEMY ARMY? WHY DO GUYS TODAY STILL STRUGGLE WITH THE THOUGHT OF WOMEN EVER BEING STRONGER OR MORE EFFECTIVE?

How starkly, then, did the tale of Deborah and Jael stand out to readers two thousand or even two hundred years ago? And let's be honest, male action heroes still outnumber female ones ten to one, so this story continues to shine as something special. The key to it, however, is to keep in mind who the true hero is.

PALM TREE PRODDING

The people of Israel were up to their old tricks, doing evil in the sight of the Lord. Their Swiss-cheese memories no longer recalled what God had done for their families in the past. If you remember the pattern from the previous chapter, you know that next God sent an enemy to oppress them, in this case Jabin, king of Canaan, along with his trusty army commander, Sisera. This wasn't an easy-going or short-lived conquest. Jabin, Sisera, and their nine hundred iron chariots—a significant military advantage—"oppressed the people of Israel cruelly for twenty years" (Judges 4:3).

The stage now set, the focus shifts to the hill country of Israel and a lazy palm tree. Under that tree sat a woman named Deborah, who was renowned for her wisdom by all the people of Israel. She sat there, day after day, listening to people's problems and disputes, giving advice, assigning punishments, and solving tricky issues. In a society whose default position was to trust warrior men for leadership, Deborah must have been a person of extraordinary insight and godly wisdom to receive this level of respect. In a peaceful time, Deborah no doubt could have spent her days solving minor disputes and keeping good order, but she lived instead in a time when Israel was suffering. More important, it was a time when the people cried to the Lord for help.

From the words in Judges, it seems likely that God had already communicated to Barak, Israel's military commander, that if he went with an army against Sisera, God would give him victory. Knowing this, Deborah summoned Barak to meet her at the palm tree. "Didn't God tell you to do this?" she asked. "Didn't He tell you to gather ten thousand people, face the enemy, and defeat Commander Sisera yourself? So, what's the holdup?"

Don't take this wrong. Barak was definitely a man of faith. Hebrews 11:32 lists him among some big-name company as a hero of the faith. But being a hero of the faith doesn't always mean making the right choices right away or with as much courage as God would like. It would be nice to say that, as soon as Deborah called him out, Barak slapped his forehead in recognition of his own foolishness and said, "Of course, I'll go." Instead, in an act that is overly cautious at best, he answers Deborah, "If you will go with me, I will go, but if you will not go with me, I will not go" (Judges 4:8). He didn't trust that the results would be as promised unless God's number one messenger at the time went with him.

THAT REMINDS ME: DEBORAH WAS NOT THE ONLY BIBLICAL LADY WHO HAD TO WORK TO GET A MAN TO DO THE RIGHT THING. ESTHER RISKED HER VERY LIFE TO GET THE KING TO SEE THE TRUTH ABOUT WHAT HIS CHIEF ADVISER WAS PLANNING FOR THE ISRAELITES. IN 1 SAMUEL 25, ABIGAIL CAN'T PREVENT HER LOSER OF A HUSBAND FROM OFFENDING DAVID, BUT SHE INTERVENES JUST IN TIME TO SAVE ALL THEIR HOUSEHOLD.

Can you visualize Deborah shaking her head in disappointment at him? This big, strong guy refused to go into battle without a wise woman to hold his hand. "Fine," she said. "I'll go, but no one's going to be talking about how great you are after we win. Instead, a woman will get all the credit for taking out Sisera." To his credit, Barak didn't question what she said. He simply put out the call for men to follow him, and ten thousand came.

Their battle plan wasn't complicated. It didn't need to be. Their secret weapon wasn't superior strategy. It was the hand of God on their side. After one more go-get-'em speech from Deborah, Barak and his men attacked the superior army and their chariots in the valley. God routed the men, rather like when He confused the chariots in the Red Sea, and Barak and his soldiers chased them down, killing every last man. All but Commander Sisera. Sisera saw where the battle was heading before it ended and made a break for it on foot. And he might have gotten away too if it wasn't for the intervention of one meddling woman.

A POUNDING HEADACHE

Exhausted, Sisera hoofed it away from the battle until he reached the tent of Jael, the wife of Heber the Kenite. He knew that Heber had made a treaty with Sisera's king, Jabin, so this should be a good place to hide until the heat blew over.

At first, this seemed like a great move. Jael was an awesome hostess. She met him warmly, invited him into the tent, gave him a nice drink of milk, and tucked the poor guy in for a nap. No doubt she'd have given him chocolate chip cookies if she had some. She even seemed willing to stand guard. Sisera figured that if she told people no one was home, they'd believe her.

And that's where he miscalculated. While Sisera was focused on the peace agreement between his king and Jael's husband, Heber the Kenite, Jael was thinking about how the Kenites had bound themselves to Israel when they traveled in the wilderness and entered the Promised Land together. The Kenites and the people of Israel had been allies for generations.

So, while the surface of the text makes it seem like there was no reason for Jael to take out Sisera, other than to spite

THAT REMINDS ME: THE KENITES WERE THE DESCENDANTS OF MOSES' FATHER-IN-LAW. THEY MADE THE FORTY-YEAR TRIP WITH ISRAEL, TYING THEIR FORTUNES TOGETHER. UPON ENTERING THE PROMISED LAND, THEY SETTLED AMONG THE TRIBE OF JUDAH. HEBER, THOUGH, HAD SEPARATED HIMSELF FROM THE OTHER KENITES AND BROKEN HIS IMPLIED AGREEMENT WITH ISRAEL AND THEIR GOD.

her husband, she was, in fact, keeping an older commitment to the people of Israel and their God. With this in mind, she turned from gracious hostess to stone-cold killer.

While Sisera slept, utterly drained from the day, Jael crept up to him, placed the tip of a tent peg against his temple, and hammered for all her worth. She wasn't taking chances. She drove the peg all the way into the ground.

This was good news for her next guest, Barak, who passed by searching for Sisera and saw his foe down for the count. From there, Israel kept up the pressure on Jabin, Sisera's king, and eventually destroyed him.

The battle won, it was celebration time. Deborah and Barak burst forth with praise, singing an epic song about the God who had saved Israel and those He used for that purpose, especially Jael, the woman who took down Israel's great enemy.

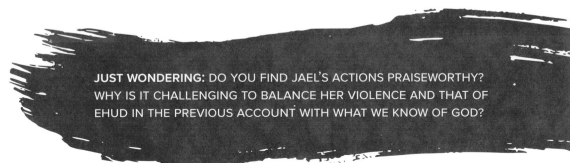

JUST WONDERING: DO YOU FIND JAEL'S ACTIONS PRAISEWORTHY? WHY IS IT CHALLENGING TO BALANCE HER VIOLENCE AND THAT OF EHUD IN THE PREVIOUS ACCOUNT WITH WHAT WE KNOW OF GOD?

WHY IS THIS IN THE BIBLE?

Some would say this story is in the Bible to make barbaric guys think twice before doing wrong by the women in their lives. While it's no doubt had that effect at times, that would be oversimplifying its significance. It would not be wrong, however, to note this as a clear case of the Lord using women to make a difference in history. Deborah and Jael were not the most likely action heroes, but that may be exactly why God chose them.

Fortunately, God can deliver freedom to His people through whatever means He sees fit. He isn't bound by our limits and imaginations. In fact, God makes a point of coming to us through less obvious routes, such as His Means of Grace (Baptism and Holy Communion). Through simple tools like water and bread and wine, He works salvation from sin in us. However, so as not to confuse us, God tells us exactly how He saves us. It is through the sacrificial life and death of His Son and the faith in Him that His Spirit works in human hearts.

Another lesson from this story is that while God wants to use us for specific purposes, if we refuse, He will still accomplish His will by another way. We don't serve God so that His will can be done. We serve Him so that we might reap the blessings of service—namely, that His will may be done through us.

Deborah, Barak, and Jael shared a common purpose in working deliverance for the people of Israel. The two women here, especially, took the lead at a time when no men were ready and willing to step up. These ladies made a difference by showing how much women were capable of when serving God in roles outside what was typical. Deborah, especially, was an outstanding role model. But just like the men in the Bible, their parts were secondary to the leading role played by God

THAT REMINDS ME: "THERE IS NEITHER JEW NOR GREEK, THERE IS NEITHER SLAVE NOR FREE, THERE IS NO MALE AND FEMALE, FOR YOU ARE ALL ONE IN CHRIST" (GALATIANS 3:28).

in this account. Deborah, like all judges and others who worked for the deliverance of God's people, foreshadowed the key man in the Bible, the God-man, Jesus Christ.

BONUS FEATURES

Women warriors: Although Deborah guided the army, she certainly wasn't a solider. Throughout history, however, many women have served with distinction in times of war. Here's a few of history's most colorful female warriors:

Queen Artemesia of Caria served as a naval commander for King Xerxes the Great of Persia. She warned Xerxes against more than one ultimately unsuccessful choice and gained renown as commander of five ships during the Battle of Salamis in the fifth century BC. Xerxes proclaimed her his greatest commander.

Fu Hao started off as one of the king's consorts during China's Shang Dynasty. Over time, she became not only a high priestess but also her nation's foremost military commander. Her importance was shown directly through the quality of treasures, such as bronze tigers, and weapons found in her tomb.

Joan of Arc is history's most famous woman of war. Claiming she'd received visions from God, young Joan led the forces of France's Charles VII to victory at Orléans. Her victory allowed Charles to be crowned and freed France from English control. Oh, and she commanded an entire nation's military at the age of 17, all before being burned at the stake at a rigged trial.

Tent types: Jael lured Sisera into her tent for some deadly business. That's not the only kind of tent out there, though.

Yurt: Portable, round tent used in Central Asia, also called a *ger.*

Tepee: Cone-shaped tent featuring animal skins placed on wooden poles. Flaps at the top of the cone release smoke.

Tupiq: Traditional Inuit tent covered in seal or caribou skin. Primarily used in the summer.

Pup tent: Small triangular tent supported by two poles, one in the front and another in the back. Often used by one or two people for camping.

Loue: Super-light Finnish open tent known for quick set-up and take-down and used for protection from wind and rain.

Wigwam: Domed tent formed with arched poles. Primarily used in the Northeastern United States and Canada.

CHAPTER 7

BRINGING DOWN THE HOUSE

Who died: Samson / lots of Philistines

How they died: Building collapse / Samson's hands and a donkey's jawbone

Why they died: Self-reliance and carelessness / opposition to God's people

When: Circa 1049 BC, around the time the Shang Dynasty ended and the Zhou Dynasty began

Where in Scripture: Judges 16

Here he is, history's first superhero, the man with lengthy locks, a tornadic temper, and more muscles than a seafood buffet (mussels are a kind of shellfish, like clams). Samson was large and in charge, and, frankly, just about unstoppable. Still, for a superhero he had an awful lot of flaws. Good thing, too, because using flawed people to do great things is one of God's specialties.

RIDDLE ME THIS

This story starts with a childless Israelite couple who were visited by the angel of the Lord and promised that God would let them have a baby.

This child would be a Nazirite from birth until death, consecrated to God's service to start saving Israel from the Philistines. As a result of his Nazirite vow, their son was to never drink alcohol, eat unclean food, or get a haircut.

JUST WONDERING: THE BIBLE IS PACKED WITH STORIES OF WOMEN WHO WANTED BUT COULDN'T HAVE CHILDREN (E.G., SARAH, HANNAH, ELIZABETH, AND RACHEL). OFTEN, THEY CRIED OUT TO GOD FOR HELP, AND HE GAVE THEM A MIRACULOUS CHILD. WHY ARE THERE SO MANY ACCOUNTS LIKE THIS? WHY ARE MOST PARENTS AND ADOPTIVE PARENTS SO GRATEFUL FOR THE CHILDREN THEY RECEIVE? IF YOU WANT, ASK A GROWN-UP YOU TRUST ABOUT THIS.

Sure enough, Samson was born, consecrated to God as a Nazirite, and grew up. In time, God blessed him with great strength and a will to deliver God's people. Oddly enough, however, the first demonstrations we see of Samson's might against the Philistines all tie into Samson's wedding.

Often impulsive, Samson probably didn't shock his parents when he insisted on marrying a cute Philistine girl rather than a godly Israelite. Eager to secure her hand, he and his folks set out to visit this girl. On the way, Samson got separated from his parents and was attacked by a lion. Samson did not run. Instead, he did what any hot-headed guy with super strength from God would do. He tore the lion apart piece by piece with his bare hands. Yeah, his bare hands.

Anyway, the marriage was arranged, and a number of days later Samson walked by the lion's carcass. What did he see? A swarm of bees making honey inside the dead lion. Feeling the munchies, Samson scooped out a major amount of honey, enough to share with his mom and dad, though he didn't say where it came from. Likely, he didn't tell them because it made them ritually unclean and, more significantly, eating food from a rotting carcass clearly violated one of his Nazirite vows to the Lord.

When Samson got to the site of the wedding feast—an event that lasted seven days—he was assigned thirty guys to be his party buddies and witnesses to the marriage. Samson, being all guy all the time, had to make things competitive, so he challenged them to solve a riddle. The losing side, either them or him, would give thirty sets of clothes to the winning side. Being bawdy Philistines, the guys said, "Bring it on!"

Samson's riddle, "Out of the eater came something to eat. Out of the strong came something sweet" (Judges 14:14), utterly confused them. Not knowing about the lion and honey, they had little chance of guessing. So, they did what any morally weak, ultra-competi-

THAT REMINDS ME: THE BIBLE SPEAKS OF WISDOM AND RIDDLES IN PROVERBS 1:5–6: "LET THE WISE HEAR AND INCREASE IN LEARNING, AND THE ONE WHO UNDERSTANDS OBTAIN GUIDANCE, TO UNDERSTAND A PROVERB AND A SAYING, THE WORDS OF THE WISE AND THEIR RIDDLES."

tive group of guys would do: they threatened Samson's bride, telling her that they'd burn her and her father's house if she didn't get the answer for them.

Samson, as we'll see again later, was a sucker for a lady crying, so he tells her. She tells the thirty companions, and they taunt Samson with the correct answer. The Spirit of the Lord came on Samson, giving him strength and using him as a weapon against the Philistines. To get the thirty outfits he owed these cheaters, he attacked a nearby Philistine city, killed thirty men, and took their clothes. Upon handing over the prize, he left in a huff, not even staying for the end of the final day of the marriage feast. Whether from spite or confusion, the bride's father then married her off to the best man.

MORE WEDDING-RELATED WOES

Once Samson cooled down, he decided to reclaim his wife. When he got to her dad's house, however, he found out about the whole best-man thing and once again blew his top. On the spot, he pledged more harm upon the Philistines.

Showing a flair for the dramatic,

JUST WONDERING: THE TEXT SAYS THEY BLACKMAILED THE BRIDE ON THE FOURTH DAY; HOWEVER, SHE BUGGED SAMSON FOR THE ANSWER FROM THE FIRST DAY, BEFORE THEY BLACKMAILED HER. WHAT DOES THIS REVEAL ABOUT HER CHARACTER AND HER LOYALTIES? ONCE THREATENED, WHAT SHOULD SHE HAVE DONE INSTEAD OF BETRAYING HER HUSBAND?

Samson rounded up three hundred foxes and tied them together in pairs, with a torch between each pair of tails. Then he set them loose in the Philistine lands, destroying their grain and orchards. The Philistines, either in punishment for causing this trouble or in a misguided attempt to appease Samson, killed Samson's "wife" and her father.

This made Samson even more ticked off, so he killed more guys, which in turn led a bigger group of Philistines to attack a town in Judah. Now, the guys in Judah were Israelites and should have stood up and cheered, "Go, Samson!" since he was their best shot at victory over the Philistines in a long time. Instead, the men of Judah went to Samson and tied him up, with his cooperation, and handed him over to the Philistines.

This, don't you know, is just what Samson was waiting for. Breaking the ropes tying him, Samson went wild, grabbing the jawbone of a donkey and killing a thousand men. He single-handedly took out a small army! And just to top it off, he made off with the gates of one of their cities when they tried to ambush him.

At this point, the Philistines had nothing but hatred for Samson. But they were also terrified of his strength, so a more subtle strategy would have to be used.

DA LYING AND DELILIAH

If you tell someone you're dating that you're deathly allergic to bees and wake up to find a couple of beehives installed outside and a beekeeper suit hanging in the closet, you might want to rethink your relationship. For some reason, this is a lesson Samson never learned.

After a fling or two, Samson's next serious relationship was with a beauty named Delilah, and she had no problem twisting her man around her little finger. That was good for her, because the Philistine lords had tasked her with finding out the secret of Samson's strength. And they promised her that if she did, they'd give her enough silver to last a solid fifteen years. Delilah may have been fond of the big guy, but she wasn't about to let this gravy train pass her by. She didn't even bother being subtle about it, straight-out begging Samson, "Please tell me where your great strength lies, and how you might be bound, that one could subdue you" (Judges 16:6).

You'd think that would set off Samson's alarm bells. She doesn't just ask, "Oooo, what makes big Sammy so strong?" No, she wants to know exactly how to take him down.

It's almost as if Samson laughed it off though. He told her that tying him up with fresh bowstrings would do the trick. She got the bowstrings, tied him up, and yelled out, "The Philistines are here!" Samson snapped the bowstrings easily, and the Philistines hiding in ambush stayed hidden.

THAT REMINDS ME: SOMEONE ELSE IN SCRIPTURE WAS OFFERED SILVER FOR THE BETRAYAL OF A PERSON CLOSE TO HIM: JUDAS. BOTH JUDAS AND DELILAH HAD REASON TO SUSPECT WHAT THEIR BETRAYALS WOULD LEAD TO.

The next time she asked him, he again embraced the game of "Trick Delilah," so he told her to use new ropes. She did, and once again, Samson had a good laugh about it. Once more she tried, this time taking his advice to braid his hair through a loom and tie it down. Still, he broke free, just as strong as ever.

Who knows what Samson was thinking at this point. Obviously, he loved—or at least seriously lusted after—Delilah, but she wasn't exactly responding the way a supportive girlfriend should. In fact, it's the exact opposite of the way God expects us to act in our relationships. We're called to cover one another's areas of weakness, making the people we care about feel safe, not threatened.

Samson's woman was looking for ways to cut him down to size and exploit his weakness, and he thought it was funny. This was truly a twisted relationship. If this was any measure of his normal honesty with Delilah, it's no wonder she harbored resentment against him.

Either Samson had a subconscious desire to be stopped or he'd pridefully forgotten where his true strength came from—and it wasn't from his hair—because the next time she asked, he told her the truth. And what do you know? She lulled him to sleep, had the barber shave his head, and woke him up in a room full of delighted Philistines. But Samson didn't tear them limb from limb. He couldn't. His strength, like his reliance on the Lord, was gone.

By being so careless with the Nazirite vow—to not cut his hair—that he'd been bound to since birth, he broke it. Samson thought he was strong, but he wasn't. Rather, God was strong through him.

PILLAR THRILLER

Determined to make him suffer, the Phi-listines gouged out Samson's eyes and set him to hard labor in prison. Eventually, this wasn't enough for them. There was a party coming up for their part-fish, part-man

THAT REMINDS ME: ONLY ONE OTHER INDIVIDUAL IN ALL OF SCRIPTURE IS CALLED A NAZIRITE FROM BIRTH: JOHN THE BAPTIST. THEY WERE BOUND BY THE SAME VOWS, AND BOTH LIVED LIVES SET ASIDE FOR SERVICE TO THE LORD. ALSO, BOTH JOHN AND SAMSON WERE ANNOUNCED BEFORE BIRTH BY ANGELIC MESSENGERS TO THEIR BARREN MOTHERS.

god, Dagon, and who would be better entertainment than the blind former strongman? That way, all the lords and ladies could have fun throwing insults his way.

Having no choice, Samson entertained them, until at last he begged the young man who led him around to put his arms on a couple pillars so he could rest. But the rest Samson was thinking of was the sleep of death.

In the time he'd been in prison, his hair had begun to grow back. More important, Samson's trust in God as the true source of his strength had returned. So, in humility, Samson sought one last chance to deliver Israel from the Philistines and to seek justice for what the Philistines had done to him as God's representative.

These weren't just any pillars Samson's hands rested on. They were the structural supports for the entire massive building. Praying to God one last time for strength, Samson pushed against the pillars, and God answered him. The pillars likely groaned as they grated against the floor and roof. Then, *crack!*, they split. The roof, which bore more partygoers, collapsed; the walls tumbled; and the entire crowd was crushed inside in a massive pile of rubble. Samson and his foes died together.

> **THAT REMINDS ME:** IN VERY DIFFERENT CIRCUM- STANCES, ANOTHER OLD TESTAMENT BUILDING COLLAPSE WAS A SOURCE OF GREAT GRIEF. SEE THE DEATH OF JOB'S CHILDREN IN JOB 1:18–19.

In the moments of his death, Samson killed more of Israel's enemies, three thousand of the Philistine leaders, than he had in all the fighting days of his life.

WHY IS THIS IN THE BIBLE?

Samson is a tempting target. He was loud. He was violent. He had horrible taste in women and questionable attitudes toward them. He was boastful and vengeful and not at all cautious about following the Lord's will. All of that is true, and yet God used him in powerful, memorable ways.

It's scary to think about someone who can see our darkest moments and every corner of our minds making a list of our faults for the world to see. Obviously, God knows all our secrets. There is no hiding from him. Yet, despite our numerous flaws, God continues to want us as workers in His kingdom. If tragically messed-up Samson can be a beacon of strength throughout history, then surely our faulty selves can be shaped into praise-giving tools as well.

We come to God as we are so He can make us how we need to be. He doesn't wait for us to be sinless to love us. He doesn't wait for us to be perfect to care for our needs. He calls us simply to rely on His strength and to ac- knowledge that even the talents we call our own are gifts solely from Him.

Both Samson and the people he killed were careless—he with his secret and they with where they let this defeated man stand. We are entrusted to give nothing but the greatest care to the chief gift entrusted to us: God's Word. We are to nurture and honor this Word within our own hearts and share it with others. Never should we be careless with our faith or with God's Word, for God is never careless with us. Indeed, God cares for the needs of both body and soul, both now and forever.

BONUS FEATURES

Musclemen: Trying to come up with real-life historical parallels for Samson is impossible. The degree of his physical might coupled with the amount of damage he did with his hands and other crude weapons is unmatched. He didn't even need a sword! The closest parallels in most people's minds involve diving into mythology and other fiction for characters such as Hercules, Beowulf, and Superman. That said, there are a few guys from history who did their best to approach Samson-like strength.

Milo of Croton enjoyed a brilliant career as a wrestler and military hero in the sixth century BC. This Greek athlete won the wrestling championship at six Olympics as well as at numerous other competitions. One feat he gained renown for was carrying a full-size bull around on his shoulders.

Scottish-born *Angus MacAskill* (1825–63) stands out among history's men of might for several reasons. For one, the Guinness Book of World Records lists him as the world's tallest natural giant—perfectly proportional with no growth abnormalities—at seven feet, nine inches tall. He weighed well over five hundred pounds of mostly muscle and was best known for lifting massive anchors to chest height.

Louis Cyr (1863–1912) earned his spot as one of history's strongest men by performing numerous feats of strength that were also well-documented—something uncommon for strongmen of the time, who liked to fudge the numbers and stories of what they'd lifted. Inspired by Milo of Croton, Louis burst into the strong-man scene by lifting an adult horse off the ground and from there battled barbells, freight trains, and enormous rocks. The career highlight for Louis, who also spent time as a police officer, was lifting a platform with eighteen men on it, almost two tons of weight!

Riddles: For a guy who loved riddles, Samson sure didn't think with his head. Still, you've got to give him points for wordplay. His is, of course, not the only famous riddle.

A. In the ancient play *Oedipus Rex*, we hear the legendary riddle of the Sphinx: "What walks on four legs when it is morning, on two legs at noon, and on three legs in the evening?"

B. An ancient Sumerian riddle translated by E. I. Gordon says, "There is a house. One enters it blind and comes out seeing. What is it?"

C. Don't forget this popular eighteenth-century English riddle:

As I was going to St. Ives,

I met a man with seven wives.

The seven wives had seven sacks.

The seven sacks had seven cats.

The seven cats had seven kits.

Kits, cats, sacks, and wives,

How many were going to St. Ives?

D. Finally, perhaps the most asked riddle of modern times and the one with the most answers: What is black and white and red all over?

A. A HUMAN. AN INFANT CRAWLS ON FOUR "LEGS," AN ADULT WALKS ON TWO LEGS, AND AN ELDERLY PERSON WALKS WITH A CANE, SYMBOLICALLY THREE LEGS.

B. A SCHOOL.

C. ONE. SINCE THE PERSON TELLING THE RIDDLE IS GOING TO ST. IVES AND MEETS THE OTHERS ON THE WAY, THE OTHERS ARE GOING AWAY FROM ST. IVES.

D. A NEWSPAPER. A PENGUIN WITH A SUNBURN. A ZEBRA WHO WRITES BESTSELLERS. A BLUSHING PANDA. YOU GET THE IDEA.

CHAPTER 8

A Sling and a Prayer

Who died: Goliath / many Philistines

How they died: Slingshot stone and beheading / general battle

Why they died: Aggression and mockery of God and David

When: Circa 1023 BC, during the time that Acastus was archon, or magistrate, of Athens, Greece

Where in Scripture: 1 Samuel 17

The timid don't make headlines. There's a reason this story isn't called "Saul and Goliath" or "Israel versus the Philistines" or "Eliab and Goliath"—Eliab being David's oldest brother, and the one who by rights should have represented Jesse's family in combat.

No, it's David and Goliath. Both names are remembered well—one as a seemingly unstoppable force of nature, and the other as the underdog shepherd boy who stopped him. Given his size and warrior's upbringing, Goliath was destined to be a headliner, but others could have stepped up to oppose him. Perhaps Saul, the king of Israel, who was experienced in war and no shorty himself. Perhaps one of David's three older brothers who were trained and serving as soldiers. For that matter, apart from pride, why didn't Saul simply reject Goliath's challenge and fight the Philistines army against army? None of them was willing to step forward boldly, trusting in their God to supply the victory. None but David.

KING ME

The days of the judges ended with the Israelites demanding that Samuel, the final true judge, appoint a king so they could be just like all the other nations. Even though God saw this for what it was—a rejection of God's own kingship over them—He told Samuel to give them a king. They would have the human leadership they wanted, but with it would come kingly demands and burdens placed upon the people. "Sign us up!" they replied.

THAT REMINDS ME: MUCH LIKE SAUL AND DAVID WERE CHOSEN BY GOD TO LEAD HIS PEOPLE, SO WAS SAMUEL CHOSEN. AS A YOUNG BOY SERVING WITH ELI IN THE TEMPLE, SAMUEL HEARD GOD CALL OUT TO HIM FOUR TIMES, AND HE ANSWERED, "SPEAK, FOR YOUR SERVANT HEARS" (1 SAMUEL 3:10). SO MAY WE REPLY TO WHATEVER SERVICE GOD CALLS US.

Israel's first chosen king sure looked the part. Taller and more handsome than any other man of Israel, Saul at first seemed a solid choice. He spoke of his tribe's humility, he prophesied by the Spirit of the Lord, and he led the people into successful battle against the Ammonites. The Israelites came together under Saul to proclaim him as their king.

But just as the people did not seek God's rule, so Saul did not continue to rule as God intended him to. The once strong king waned in faith, and his offenses piled up: making an unlawful sacrifice, not trusting God to lead him to victory, making a foolish vow, and greedily disobeying God's command to destroy the enemy's livestock. God would have no more of it, so He sent Samuel in secret to anoint a new king to one day replace Saul.

And when Samuel came to the household of Jesse in Bethlehem, he knew the next king was near. Jesse's seven sons before him were strong and fit. Surely God had chosen one of them. But one at a time, they passed Samuel, and God whispered to Samuel, "Not him. Not him. Not this one. Not him."

"Is that it?" Samuel asked Jesse.

"My youngest is out with the sheep," said Jesse. That youngest son, as you know, was David, and he hurried up to his father and Samuel.

THAT REMINDS ME: ALTHOUGH THE ELDEST SON TYPICALLY RECEIVED THE GREATEST HONOR, POSITION, AND INHERITANCE, GOD OFTEN WORKS IN UNEXPECTED WAYS, AS HE DID WITH DAVID. MUCH LIKE JOSEPH OF OLD, DAVID WAS HONORED ABOVE AND BEYOND HIS OLDER BROTHERS BUT ALSO PROVIDED FOR HIS FAMILY'S HONOR AND POSSESSIONS.

"That's him," God reassured Samuel. So Samuel anointed him with oil right then and there. Whether David or his family knew what the anointing meant is questionable, but Samuel knew. This David, son of Jesse, would one day be king. Notable, too, at this point is that David was also so gifted a musician that he alone could soothe Saul's spirit. For this ability, he made the acquaintance of the king and served, at least sometimes, as Saul's armor bearer.

ANYBODY? ANYBODY?

Those Philistines who were a thorn in Israel's side in Samson's day continued to struggle with Israel in the time of Saul. So it was that David, who'd been at home tending to his father's flocks, brought care packages from his father to his three oldest brothers, who served as soldiers in Saul's army. Lined up on either side of the same valley, the two armies were prepared for war but had not yet engaged in battle.

Instead, as David discovered, a different offer had been made. A heavily armed and armored mountain of a man named Goliath of Gath had roared out his challenge. If any man of Israel would fight him one-on-one, that would decide which army won without the need for any more bloodshed. The loser's side would become the servants of the winner's side.

With a proportionally giant sword, shield, and javelin, the nine-foot-tall Goliath knew he could defeat anyone sent against him. But neither Saul nor a single one of his manly warriors had the courage or the faith in God to accept Goliath's challenge. Also, it's not like Goliath made this challenge just once or twice. Every day for forty days, his voice boomed with scorn for the Israelites. Every day for forty days, no answer came from the Israelite camp.

When David heard that no one had taken up Goliath's challenge, he was furious. How could they not defend the glory of God's people? It was especially unthinkable because Saul had offered great riches and the hand of one of his daughters in marriage to whoever would face Goliath. Still, no one was volunteering. After forty days, this wasn't just momentary panic. It was deep-seated fear of Goliath that outweighed their trust in the God of Israel.

"Fine!" said David, and he marched into Saul's headquarters and announced, "I'll do it."

JUST WONDERING: WHEN DAVID ASKED ABOUT GOLIATH, DAVID'S OLDEST BROTHER, ELIAB, CHEWED DAVID OUT, CLAIMING HE'D ABANDONED THE SHEEP OUT OF AN EVIL DESIRE TO WATCH THE BATTLE. CLEARLY, ELIAB WAS WRONG ON SEVERAL POINTS. WHY IS IT SO EASY TO ACCUSE BROTHERS AND SISTERS OF WRONGDOING? WHY IS IT HARD TO ADMIT WHEN THEY'RE BEING WISER THAN WE ARE?

PREP WORK

So, this young guy, certainly under age 20 and not a trained soldier, comes to Saul and says, "I'll fight the unbeatable giant." Saul's first answer should have been "No way!" No way could he afford to put the fate of his nation in the hands of a kid.

This is the moment where shame should've kicked in, where Saul's next words should have been "I'm the king! I'm going to fight him! I'm the biggest, tallest man in Israel, and it's my job to protect the people." Rather, Saul weakly argues, "You sure, kid? This guy's been a super warrior since he was your age."

Saul folded after David's argument: "I watch the sheep for my dad, and I've killed lions and bears. I'll kill this nasty Philistine just like I killed them." Then, just to lock it in, David said, "'The LORD who delivered me from the paw of the bear will deliver me from the hand of this Philistine.' And Saul said to David, 'Go and the LORD be with you!'" (1 Samuel 17:37).

Even if he was trying to trust this boy to win, Saul was still trusting in the things he knew, like armor and swords. He loaded David up with his own helmet and chain mail, something that at least would let Saul claim some credit if David should get lucky and win. But even that didn't feel right to David. He took them off. If he was going to face Goliath, it would be with the tools God had trained him to use. He held only his staff, his sling, and five smooth stones he chose from the brook. Loaded up, he went to fight Goliath.

"AM I A DOG, UNDERDOG?"

Imagine how you would feel if you were Goliath. Your whole life has made it abundantly clear that there is no one more horrifying than yourself, and after your fair share of battles, here's your big moment. Day after day, the pesky Israelites cower in terror as you shout across the valley for one of them to be a man and face you. After forty days of this, you know there's no one even close to your stature in Israel. Still, there are plenty of experienced warriors who could take you on. Better yet, King Saul, who, with his son Jonathan had defeated your Philistine people earlier, could step forward. What better way to cement your reputation than with the head of Israel's king propped up on the end of your javelin?

Instead, when the moment finally comes and a challenger approaches, you get a kid—okay, a young man. But he's young, and he's not in armor. No sword, no shield, nothing. Surely this is a bad Israelite joke. Still, he comes closer, and your anger devours you. It's an insult, a travesty. Mighty Goliath deserves a mighty challenger, and instead you get a mere boy with a staff and a sling.

It's no wonder then that Goliath's next words were "Am I a dog, that you come to me with sticks?" (17:43). Even if David were tall, the difference between them was like the difference between a grown-up and a six-year-old. Seeing this was not the epic battle he'd been waiting for, Goliath called upon his false gods to curse David. Then he taunted, "Come to me, and I will give your flesh to the birds of the air and to the beasts of the field" (v. 44).

David's reply should have been jarring to Goliath. Not a frightened boy, this young man of God spoke with confidence about what would happen and whose God would triumph. In essence he said, "You come to me with warrior's weapons, but I come in the name of the mighty God of Israel. By His power, you will be the one cut down, and your army's flesh will feed the birds and beasts so all may know that Israel's Lord is God."

THAT REMINDS ME: THE BIBLE IS STUFFED WITH STORIES OF GOD ACHIEVING GREAT VICTORIES BY UNEXPECTED MEANS. IN JUDGES 7, WE HEAR THE AMAZING STORY OF HOW GOD USED GIDEON'S SMALL ARMY OF MEN CARRYING TRUMPETS IN ONE HAND AND JARS WITH TORCHES IN THE OTHER TO DEFEAT A GREATER FOE. THIS IN TURN REMINDS US OF JOSHUA MARCHING AROUND JERICHO AND HOW THE LORD USED TRUMPETS AND SHOUTS TO BRING THE WALL DOWN.

They both hurried to meet each other in combat. But it was a short fight. David put a stone in his sling, hurled it around, and whacked Goliath right in the forehead. The stone hit him so hard that it sank into his head. Whether Goliath had misadjusted his helmet or left it off entirely since his foe was so puny, we can't be sure. But there was no mistaking the deadly power of David's stone once it impacted. Goliath tumbled face-first to the ground. Though we don't know exactly how fast the stone was going, there is a long history of slung stones being used to lethal effect in warfare, and a speed of at least sixty miles per hour is likely. Goliath literally never knew what hit him.

Just to make sure the giant was dead for good and to prove it to both armies, David ran forward and took Goliath's own massive sword. Showing his own strength to handle the huge weapon, David cut off Goliath's head. It's easy to see why the Philistine army's next move was to run away in terror. Many Philistines fell and were killed that day. The Lord had used David to save Israel.

WHY IS THIS IN THE BIBLE?

Lion-killer. Strongman Samson and shepherd boy David could both make this claim. And while there are a few other things they have in common—such as their service to God and interest in wordplay—it's pretty hard to confuse the two. In fact, when it comes to pure brute force, Samson seems a much closer match for Goliath than little David was.

One key difference, until right before the end, is that Samson gave the impression of someone who trusted primarily in his own strength, whereas David made it perfectly clear that his strength and his victory came solely from the Lord. While God can use anyone, He takes special interest in humble hearts that seek His will.

These are the kind of hearts God longs to create within us: hearts that trust in Him no matter the circumstances or the immediate obstacles. Certainly, the story of David and Goliath isn't about fighting skill or defying the odds. Like so many others, it's simply about faith. And not faith in the strength of muscles or the quality of weapons. Faith in the power of the almighty God to protect and serve those who put their trust in Him.

Much like Saul, the Israelite army, and Goliath all saw David as an underdog, unlikely to win, so the world sees us as underdogs against the forces that oppose us. And on our own, we are underdogs. The devil, death, and our own sinful natures appear as undefeatable forces for people so frail and flawed.

JUST WONDERING: WHILE HUMILITY IS ESSENTIAL FOR EVERY CHRISTIAN, BEING TOO TIMID CAN STAND IN THE WAY OF ACHIEVING OUR GOALS AND SHARING THE GOSPEL. WHEN HAS TIMIDITY GOTTEN IN YOUR WAY WHEN FACED WITH AN OPPORTUNITY TO WITNESS? HOW CAN YOU TELL THE DIFFERENCE BETWEEN BEING PROUD AND BEING BOLD, BETWEEN BEING TIMID AND BEING HUMBLE?

However, the truth in Christ is that we are far from underdogs. Just as David approached battle well-prepared by his encounters with lions and bears, equipped with a deadly weapon, and armed with the name of the all-powerful God, so do we go forth. Our enemies are weaklings compared to God, who has saved us time and again by the unbeatable power of His Son, Jesus Christ, who died on the cross and rose again so that we are tied to His victory. No longer underdogs, we can face all the giants in our lives with courage and confidence.

BONUS FEATURES

I rock: In the story of David and Goliath, most of the focus is rightly on David and the deliverance God granted through him. Still, those five stones he grabbed, especially the one he slung at Goliath, certainly rocked the future of the Israelites. Here are other memorable stones from across the ages:

The Blarney Stone: This chunk of blue rock resides in the battlements of Blarney Castle near Cork, Ireland. Although there are conflicting stories about the origin of the stone, one legend has remained the same. If a person kisses the stone, which can be done by leaning backward in a tough position, he or she will supposedly receive the gift of eloquence, knowing exactly the words to say at all times.

Plymouth Rock: The claim is that this rock is what John Alden first stepped on when disembarking from the Mayflower with the rest of the Pilgrims in 1620. However, this is unlikely as the stone now known as Plymouth Rock was consecrated in 1774, and since then has lost at least half of its mass to tourists who have chipped away at it.

Stonehenge: This stone monument has more stories about its origin, uses, and timeline than any other group of stones around. What is clear is that Stonehenge is at least thousands of years old, was added to over the years, and is partly comprised of giant stones that came from more than a hundred miles away—an astounding achievement in ancient times. Whether you think Stonehenge was a place for religious rituals, an astronomer's paradise, a giant clock, or an alien landing pad, it's stone-cold awesome.

The Rosetta Stone: This portion of an Egyptian inscription was chipped out of a temple and used in a fort. Its true significance isn't so much what it says as what it helped Egyptologists understand. The hieroglyphs on the Rosetta Stone proved essential in deciphering this previously untranslatable writing system.

The stone in front of Jesus' tomb: This stone is most famous for what it didn't do. It didn't stay in place blocking Jesus' place of burial. This let visitors to the tomb see that Christ was no longer buried inside.

Sling power: There's no doubt that slings are both underestimated and deadly. Many in the past have realized their full value. Greek General Xenophon specifically recruited slingers to counter Persian archers and slingers. The Romans gladly employed slingers, whose weapons at times could attain greater range and accuracy than those of archers. Ancient slings were even found in the tomb of old King Tut of Egypt.

The Bible, too, mentions slings in other places:

Judges 20:16 mentions seven hundred left-handed men who could sling a stone at a hair without missing.

In *1 Chronicles 12:2,* David's warriors were joined by a group of Benjaminites who could shoot arrows and sling stones with either hand.

In *2 Kings 3:25,* slingers played a key role in defeating the Moabites.

CHAPTER 9

HANGING AROUND AND GETTING THE POINT

Who died: Absalom / many soldiers

How they died: Caught by head or hair; javelins to the heart / warfare

Why they died: Pride and rebellion

When: Circa 973 BC, during the reign of King Hiram of Tyre

Where in Scripture: 2 Samuel 18

Getting a haircut isn't always a good idea—just ask Samson—but it could have been a lifesaver for Absalom. Perhaps a better takeaway from the life of David's son Absalom is this: family can be complicated.

Just think about all the times your family has been filled with craziness, mistakes, and miscommunication. Even the most loving, listening families face hurdles to daily kindness. If you're a rich and powerful monarch or his son, the complications and the results of missteps can get really wild.

The Bible is jam-packed with stories of dysfunctional families who can't seem to get along, and often it's simply baffling. Heroes of the faith, clearly good guys and gals whom God blessed and used to do great things fell flat on their faces when it came to family matters. Take Jacob's family alone, and you get a mother helping one son trick his brother and father, a son and an uncle scheming against each other, two sisters in a rivalry with each other, and brother feuding with brother. And that's without even mentioning Jacob's messed-up kids: Joseph and his brothers. Even with the purest of hearts, the ugly pattern repeats.

FATHER AND SON

For the true story of Absalom, the best place to start is with the relationship between father and son. It seemed impossible that Absalom's father, good King David, would be anything other than a first-class parent. After all, apart from that one mistake with Bathsheba (the woman whose husband he killed so he could have her for himself), David was practically perfect, right? I mean, the Bible says he was "a man after [God's] own heart" (1 Samuel 13:14).

It doesn't matter who you are. Sin is still part of your world, and it is still present in your family. Heroes of the faith are no exception. And that "small" mistake with Bathsheba, taking as his wife a woman who was wed to another, caused major ripples. For starters, the death of the first son of David and Bathsheba. For another, a prophecy in 2 Samuel 12 that evil would rise up against David from within his own family. Boy, did it ever.

The tale of corruption within David's family is complicated, but here's the quick version. David's son by one wife assaulted and dishonored the daughter of another wife. This daughter's brother, Absalom, was enraged at his half-brother and miffed that his father did nothing about it. So Absalom began scheming, murdered his half-brother, made up lies about his father, and encouraged the people to follow him instead of daddy David. All Absalom's plans took a while to put into action, but they worked, and King David fled the capital, Jerusalem, with many of his supporters now firmly on Absalom's side. Meanwhile, Absalom strolled into Jerusalem and took everything that belonged to his father.

ABSOLUTELY ABSALOM

A few notes about Absalom: besides having it out for David, he was extremely handsome, vain, and devoted to taking over the kingdom, no matter the cost. Perhaps he saw justice in his efforts to usurp his father's reign. After all, Saul accused David of doing the same to him— never mind that God chose David for kingship and that David treated Saul with the highest respect, even while Saul was trying to kill him. Absalom knew what he wanted, and he was determined to get it.

THAT REMINDS ME: AS DAVID'S POPULARITY INCREASED, KING SAUL'S JEALOUSY ERUPTED INTO A DESIRE TO KILL HIM. ONCE, WHILE HUNTING DOWN DAVID WITH HIS ARMY, SAUL WENT INTO A CAVE FOR A BATHROOM BREAK. SAUL DIDN'T KNOW THAT DAVID AND HIS MEN WERE HIDING DEEP WITHIN THE CAVE AND COULD HAVE EASILY KILLED HIM. INSTEAD, DAVID CUT A CORNER FROM SAUL'S ROBE AS PROOF THAT HE MEANT THE CURRENT KING NO HARM. AND THIS WASN'T THE ONLY TIME DAVID SPARED SAUL'S LIFE. SEE 1 SAMUEL 24 AND 26.

Just as everything was going his way, Absalom got some suggestions, starting with great advice from someone who seemed to know everything and whose plan was brilliant. Then he got some not-so-great advice from one of David's friends. Fueled by his desire for kingship, Absalom took the bad advice, and David escaped, giving his army the chance to ride out into battle. In an extremely bloody encounter over rough ground covered with trees, David's forces defeated Absalom's. More than twenty thousand men died, killed by sword and the harsh terrain. The text even says, "And the forest devoured more people that day than the sword" (2 Samuel 18:8).

That's when Absalom's luck went from bad to worse. While riding on a mule—a symbol of kingship—he got caught in a tree by his head, probably his long hair. The mule rode on, but Absalom was stuck.

THAT REMINDS ME: LITERATURE SUCH AS J. R. R. TOLKIEN'S *THE LORD OF THE RINGS* FEATURES TREES ENGAGED IN BATTLE. TOLKIEN'S TREELIKE ENTS MIGHT MOVE SLOWLY, BUT THEY HAVE GREAT POWER. IN SHAKESPEARE'S *MACBETH*, MALCOLM'S SOLDIERS MAKE AN ENTIRE FOREST APPEAR TO MOVE BY CUTTING DOWN LARGE BOUGHS FROM THE TREES AND HIDING BEHIND THEM.

Now David, even after all the cruddy stuff his son had done, ordered the army to be gentle with Absalom. There are two ways to take this: either David rightly still desired to forgive his son, or David was too soft-hearted to let Absalom receive the discipline and punishment his terrible acts deserved. Either way, when one of David's men saw Absalom hanging helplessly from the tree, he did not kill him. Instead, the man went to Joab, the general of David's army, and told him.

Warrior Joab was royally miffed at the guy for not killing Absalom, but the wise man said he wasn't about to disobey David's command to be gentle. Plus, he guessed that if had killed Absalom, Joab would have faked anger and let David punish the man. Joab rode off in a huff to where Absalom still dangled from the tree. Ever practical, Joab grabbed three javelins on the spot and plunged them through Absalom's still-beating heart. And just to make sure the job was done, ten of Joab's guys played piñata with Absalom until he was fully and finally dead.

JUST WONDERING: BOTH JESUS AND ABSALOM DIED HANGING FROM A TREE. WHILE ABSALOM EARNED HIS CURSE, JESUS DID NOT. HE, IN FACT, SAVED US BY CHOOSING TO BE CURSED FOR US. "CHRIST REDEEMED US FROM THE CURSE OF THE LAW BY BECOMING A CURSE FOR US—FOR IT IS WRITTEN, 'CURSED IS EVERYONE WHO IS HANGED ON A TREE'" (GALATIANS 3:13). HOW ARE JESUS AND ABSALOM SIMILAR? IN WHAT WAYS IS ABSALOM AN OPPOSITE, OR ANTITYPE, OF CHRIST?

Then, because even that wasn't shameful enough, Joab ordered Absalom's body to be thrown into a large pit in the forest. On top of the corpse, they piled a massive heap of stones, so everyone could see exactly where Absalom was buried. Joab wasn't about to let this enemy ever come back to trouble the kingdom again.

MIXED MESSAGES AND A MOURNING MONARCH

The story could end there if it weren't for the mixed-up stuff that happened in the aftermath. Since they didn't have cell phones or the Internet in those days, getting messages across a distance took some time. Hours after the fact, David still didn't know that his army had won or that Absalom was dead.

Excited mainly about the military victory, Ahimaaz, the well-known son of Zadok the priest, told Joab he wanted to go right away to let David know they'd won. But Joab knew how touchy David was about Absalom and was concerned the king wouldn't take the news well, so he wouldn't let Ahimaaz go, likely for fear the man would be punished. Instead, he sent a Cushite, possibly a slave, to tell David what he had witnessed. Still, Ahimaaz wanted to go. Either he wanted to be the one to share what he thought was good news or he wanted the king to get it as soon as possible. Ahimaaz knew good and well that he was the fastest messenger around. Reluctantly, Joab let him go too.

It turns out Ahimaaz was right about his speed because he arrived before the Cushite. Ahimaaz bowed before David and proclaimed that the king's enemies had been defeated. But David considered himself a father first and king second, so he wanted to know only about Absalom. Interestingly, Ahimaaz, who'd been so concerned about getting news to the king, suddenly had memory loss, acting as though Absalom's fate wasn't known before Ahimaaz began his run. When the Cushite arrived, the king again asked, "'Is it well with the young man Absalom?' And the Cushite answered, 'May the enemies of my lord the king and all who rise up against you for evil be like that young man'" (2 Samuel 18:32). But David had no joy in the victory. Instead, he turned aside and wept, wishing that he had died in his son's place.

The king's mourning was not quiet or short-lived. All the people heard it or heard about it, and many did not take it well. Knowing this, General Joab entered the scene again. In an act that was incredibly bold, Joab chastised the king up one side and down the other. He reminded David that in defeating Absalom, the lives of David's other children, David's servants, and his supporters had been saved as well. David's tears for Absalom, while understandable, were offensive to all those people Absalom had sought to kill.

Wisely, David listened, and went back to speak kindly to those who'd supported him.

WHY IS THIS IN THE BIBLE?

This is the tale of three men: Absalom, David, and Joab. Each holds his own lessons to share.

Absalom teaches what can go wrong when a family relationship is spoiled by arrogance, miscommunication, and entitlement. Absalom possessed some impressive qualities for a son and a potential king.

1. He was bold to speak what he thought was right.
2. He was charismatic and knew how to gather people together under his leadership.
3. He was patient in letting his plans for revenge take time.
4. He should even be commended for his willingness to seek advice— many a leader takes advice only from himself.

Of course, each of these positive traits had a dark side.

1. Absalom's boldness showed itself as impertinence. And he was a poor judge of what was truly right.
2. His charisma fed directly into his overblown ego and vanity.

3. His patience early on gave way to impatience. Consider that David lived only a few more years after these events. If his sin hadn't taken charge, Absalom could have sucked up his pride and become king the natural way. Absalom was popular, and Solomon's ascent as king was by no means locked in at this point.

4. Seeking advice is good, but Absalom had abysmal judgment on which advice to follow.

David, over and over again, in his relationship with Absalom, radiated forgiveness and unconditional love. No matter what his son's offenses, David was ready to show mercy and kindness. In many ways this is a fabulous example for earthly fathers and a beautiful image of our heavenly Father's unending love for us. However, it's not the whole story. David's mercy toward Absalom was unbalanced because he refused to discipline his son.

God does not merely serve as our Father because He loves and forgives us, but also because He reprimands and redirects us away from evil. Even though we are incapable of perfectly following God's guidance, He still shows us our sin so that we will run from that and into His arms of love. David, for all his wonderful attributes, failed to show Absalom the severity of his wrongdoing, leaving Absalom to falsely think himself righteous and not in need of help.

The third leg of this story is the trickiest. It's hard to pinpoint Joab's morality in this account. He's definitely a loyal supporter of David and a defender of his kingship. He comes across as a competent leader and shows a form of wisdom. On the other hand, he blatantly disregards David's command to be gentle with Absalom and takes his time sending David the full story of what happened. On the other, other hand, it must have been infuriating for a military man like Joab to see David repeatedly showing unwarranted kindness to the traitor who'd torn apart the kingdom in war.

Perhaps a good lesson from Joab is to take care in how you follow those in authority over you, how you instruct those under you, and how you balance what is practical with what is morally right. As Joab surely knew, none of those tasks should be taken lightly or performed without careful thought and reflection on God's ultimate leadership.

One final point from all three is the importance of relying on God in all our human relationships. Even the very best ones bear the cracks of sin and can benefit from the strengthening power of God's Word. Our bonds with others can become more authentic and unassailable only when we rely on God to preserve us and those we care about. His guidance about how to balance love and Law when speaking to loved ones is invaluable.

Just as Christ restored our relationship with our heavenly Father, so He works to build us up in community with one another.

BONUS FEATURES

Warrior-poet: A man mighty with actions and graceful with words, David possessed many talents. Roughly half of the psalms are attributed to David, including Psalm 3, which bears the following note: "A Psalm of David, when he fled from Absalom his son."

PSALM 3

"O LORD, HOW MANY ARE MY FOES!
    MANY ARE RISING AGAINST ME;
MANY ARE SAYING OF MY SOUL,
    THERE IS NO SALVATION FOR HIM IN GOD.
BUT YOU, O LORD, ARE A SHIELD ABOUT ME,
    MY GLORY, AND THE LIFTER OF MY HEAD.
I CRIED ALOUD TO THE LORD,
    AND HE ANSWERED ME FROM HIS HOLY HILL.
I LAY DOWN AND SLEPT;
    I WOKE AGAIN, FOR THE LORD SUSTAINED ME.
I WILL NOT BE AFRAID OF MANY THOUSANDS OF PEOPLE
    WHO HAVE SET THEMSELVES AGAINST ME ALL AROUND.
ARISE, O LORD!
    SAVE ME, O MY GOD!
FOR YOU STRIKE ALL MY ENEMIES ON THE CHEEK;
    YOU BREAK THE TEETH OF THE WICKED.
SALVATION BELONGS TO THE LORD;
    YOUR BLESSING BE ON YOUR PEOPLE!"

Getting the point: Being skewered is not on most people's top-ten list of peaceful ways to die. Being stabbed through the heart, lungs, kidneys, and other organs would cause major bleeding, make breathing difficult, and hurt like the dickens. And looking down to see the shaft of the weapons still sticking out of you has to be a horrific sight.

Despite this, there are people who, over time, have trained their bodies to survive being skewered in specific ways. Sometimes called human pincushions, they were a staple of early twentieth-century freak shows. Mirin Dajo was known to have assistants push swords through his body many times a day, with audiences standing as close as they wished to verify everything. He even swallowed razor blades and crushed glass to no ill effect. In the end, though, he died days after a hospital removed a steel needle he'd swallowed.

JUST TO BE CLEAR: Do not try to swallow sharp objects or stab yourself or anyone else! You will be hurt or worse.

Skewer guide:
Good Things to Put on Skewers
Shish kebabs
Marshmallows
Yarn (knitting needles resemble skewers)
Certain candles
Hot dogs
Strawberries

Bad Things to Put on Skewers
Books
Pets
Pudding
Anything belonging to your mom
Balloons
Fireworks

CHAPTER 10

BAAL GOES DOWN THE TOILET

Who died: Prophets of Baal

How they died: General slaughter

Why they died: Worship of false gods

When: Circa 871 BC, eight years before legend says the city of Bath in England was founded

Where in Scripture: 1 Kings 18

Elijah was the superstar of prophets. Big miracles? Check. Dramatic confrontations? Check. Endless oppression and death threats? Check and check. Raising the dead? Yup, that too. Elijah did it all. Or rather, he served the One who did it all.

It's fair to say that Elijah's confrontation with the prophets of Baal was the Super Bowl of prophetic competitions, a must-see event, and the most dramatic tale of Elijah, who was certainly at the top of his game.

CALLING ALL PROPHETS

Three and a half years earlier, Elijah had appeared before evil King Ahab of Israel and announced that there would be a severe drought. Elijah warned

that rain would not be a natural occurrence during this time and would come again only by God's command. This drought is often interpreted as a judgment on Ahab and his wife, Jezebel, who were, bar none, the most wicked, ungodly rulers of Israel yet. Ahab and Jezebel served false gods and encouraged God's people to do the same.

During the intervening three and a half years, water was extremely hard to come by. Elijah survived only because God provided food and drink directly for him. Meanwhile, the people suffered, the land was dry, and Ahab fumed over the state of his kingdom. Then came the day that God decided to end the drought. He told Elijah to show himself to Ahab and that He would then send rain again to the region.

Elijah did as instructed. However, he was not welcomed kindly by Ahab, and thus the king missed out on hearing about the impending rain. Instead, Ahab said, "Is it you, you troubler of Israel?" (1 Kings 18:17). Elijah threw it right back at him, basically saying, "Oh, yeah, which one of us has been a pain for Israel? You're the one who turned your back on God to follow Baal. So, great king, you're going to gather the people of Israel at Mount Carmel,

THAT REMINDS ME: TO THE CANAANITES, BAAL WAS THE GOD OF THE CROPS, AND
ASHERAH THE GODDESS OF FERTILITY. THE LENGTHY DROUGHT IN A TIME WHEN THESE
CANAANITE DEITIES WERE BEING PROMOTED IN ISRAEL WAS A SLAP IN THE FACE AGAINST
THEIR ALLEGED POWER OVER NATURE. THE CROPS, THE LAND, AND ITS CREATURES
SHOWED LITTLE GROWTH AND FERTILITY. THESE FALSE GODS WERE SAID TO TRADE GOOD
WEATHER AND GOOD HARVESTS FOR PRAYERS, SACRIFICES, AND SINFUL RITUALS. DURING
THIS DROUGHT, THEY RECEIVED THEIR DUE BUT GAVE NOTHING BACK.

along with the 450 prophets of Baal and the 400 prophets of Asherah whom
your wife pampers. I'll be waiting."

A BATHROOM FOR BAAL

It's impressive that Ahab went along with Elijah's demands. They weren't
exactly friends, and the last thing Ahab wanted was for Elijah to cause
more trouble. Most likely, Ahab figured this would be a good chance to
silence Elijah once and for all. With hundreds of Baal's prophets lined up
against him, Elijah seemed destined to lose. Then, the prophets and the
people could "take care of" Elijah. That would be much more effective than
a private execution.

So, the people of Israel, the pagan prophets, and Ahab all gathered
together at Mount Carmel, not knowing what to expect next, when out
swaggered Elijah. He walked right up to the Israelite crowd and laid into
them for their lack of loyalty to God: "How long will you go limping between
two different opinions? If the LORD is God, follow Him; but if Baal, then
follow him" (1 Kings 18:21). And in that moment, the people proved how
true Elijah's words were, because they didn't argue with him or shout loyalty
to God or to Baal. Instead, they stood silent. The people of Israel were so
frustratingly indecisive that even being reprimanded didn't make them take
a stand.

THAT REMINDS ME: REVELATION 3:15–16 SHARES JESUS' WORDS FOR A CONGREGATION
WHOSE INDIFFERENCE HAS SIMILARITIES TO THAT OF THE ISRAELITES IN THIS STORY: "I
KNOW YOUR WORKS: YOU ARE NEITHER COLD NOR HOT. WOULD THAT YOU WERE EITHER
COLD OR HOT! SO, BECAUSE YOU ARE LUKEWARM, AND NEITHER HOT NOR COLD, I WILL
SPIT YOU OUT OF MY MOUTH."

It was time for action, and Elijah knew just what it would take to shake the people out of their noncommittal attitude: a contest. The teams were obvious. On one side were the 450 prophets of Baal. On the other side stood Elijah, all by himself. The other prophets of the Lord were still in hiding, lest they be killed by Jezebel and Ahab.

The rules, too, were straightforward. Two bulls would be provided, from which team Baal would have first pick. They were to cut it in pieces and lay it on some wood they'd prepared, but they could not start the fire. Elijah would do the same. Then each side could call out to their deity of choice, and the one who answered by lighting the fire would be declared the true God.

Apparently, this pleased the people because they said, "That sounds great." The lazy Israelites were relieved that they did not have to decide for themselves. And the prophets of Baal were probably thinking that this Elijah guy was a real sucker, because not only was the wood very dry from the lack of rain, but he was letting their 450-man squad go first. They could win this thing without Elijah even taking a turn.

That was pretty much the last happy moment any of Baal's prophets enjoyed. After preparing the bull and the wood, they danced around the would-be sacrifice all morning, crying out, "O Baal, answer us!" (1 Kings 18:26), but there was no voice from heaven, no fire, no answer at all. They kept going and going and going, limping in circles helplessly until, at noon, Elijah couldn't hold the sarcasm in any longer: "Cry aloud, for he is a god. Either he is musing, or he is relieving himself, or he is on a journey, or perhaps he is asleep and must be awakened" (v. 27). Yup, Elijah went there, suggesting Baal couldn't help because he was on the potty in the little deity's room.

JUST WONDERING: ELIJAH IS FAR FROM POLITE IN HIS MOCKERY OF BAAL'S PROPHETS. WHAT'S THE DIFFERENCE BETWEEN ELIJAH'S VERBAL BARBS AND THE ONES WE THROW OUT AT BROTHERS AND SISTERS AND FRIENDS? DO YOU THINK, IN THIS INSTANCE, THAT GOD APPROVED OF ELIJAH'S WORDS?

Getting desperate, Baal's prophets cut them-selves with swords and lances, gushing out blood in hopes of drawing sympathy from Baal. And though they didn't stop shouting, "raving," the Bible says, "no one paid attention" (v. 29). This, of course, is because there was no one, no Baal, to pay attention.

GOD LIGHTS IT UP

The time for mockery was past, and Elijah was all business as he called the people to all gather round, nice and close. If ever there was a group of people in need of a sign to make them do the right thing, it was this group of Israelites, so Elijah wasn't about to let any of them miss what was about to happen.

First, he repaired the foundation of the old altar to the Lord that had been destroyed there, perhaps by Ahab and Jezebel themselves. Then, re-minding the Israelites of their history, he took twelve stones—one for each tribe of the sons of Jacob—and built up the altar in the Lord's name. Keep in mind, too, that this is not a tiny classroom altar. This was a full-size deal, big enough to hold an entire bull and all the wood beneath it.

The next move, though, was unexpected. He made a significant trench around the altar. This might have caused the people or the nearby prophets of Baal to wonder what he was up to. A trench wasn't part of Altar Building 101. Before they could think about it too hard, though, he got back on track, stacking the wood on the altar. Then, he sliced up the bull and put it in place on the wood.

And just when they thought he was ready to pray, he threw the people for another loop. He told them to fill four huge jars with water and pour them on the bull and the wood. Perhaps thinking he was loony, they did it. Then he had them do it a second time and a third time, until the water swamped the whole altar area and filled the trench to the top.

Elijah knew how important this moment was to the faith of the Israelite people in front of him and to their descendants in years to come. By the time he was done, the purpose of the water was clear. There would be no tricks, no games, no deceit. Elijah wasn't going to fumble a lighter behind his back and pin the credit on God. Nope, he'd made the challenge as tough as it could be, and there was no way any mortal man could claim responsibility.

JUST WONDERING: JUDGES 6:36–40 CONTAINS THE ACCOUNT OF GIDEON ASKING GOD TO PROVE HIMSELF BY PERFORMING A MIRACLE. THEN, WHEN THAT WASN'T GOOD ENOUGH, HE ASKED FOR A SECOND MIRACLE. WHAT'S THE DIFFERENCE BETWEEN ASKING FOR A MIRACLE AND SINFULLY PUTTING GOD TO THE TEST? IN OUR ELIJAH ACCOUNT, WAS THE WATER MEANT AS AN EXTRA TEST FOR GOD?

That's when Elijah began his prayer to the God of Abraham, Isaac, and Jacob, pleading for Him to show Himself as the only God in Israel and to claim again the hearts of these lukewarm Israelites as His own. Instantly, fire sizzled from the sky, devouring not only the bull and the wood, but the stones and the dust and every drop of water within that trench. This caused a second miracle, the miracle of faith within the human heart, as these unemotional people fell on their faces and said, "The LORD, He is God; the LORD, He is God" (v. 39) At last they believed. One man versus 450: uneven odds by any count. But now the people of Israel knew what Elijah had known all along: even 450 opponents are nothing when one man has the power of the one true God on his side. So, striking while the opportunity was ripe, Elijah commanded the people to grab the prophets of Baal and bring them to a nearby brook. There, Elijah and the people slaughtered them.

And yes, right after this event, rain poured from the sky over the land, ending the long drought.

THAT REMINDS ME: FOLLOWING THIS ACCOUNT IS A MEAL AND A RACE OF SORTS BETWEEN ELIJAH AND AHAB. READ MORE ABOUT IT IN 1 KINGS 18:41–46.

WHY IS THIS IN THE BIBLE?

Oh, how easy it is to be apathetic, to not care one way or another. The Israelites of Elijah's day tried to play around with false gods and false teachings, figuring that as long as they didn't fully commit, the God of Israel would take them back. It was kind of like God insurance, like saying, "I'll put fifty dollars on God and fifty on Baal, and at worst I'll break even." They thought half a heart should be good enough for God.

God, however, doesn't accept anything less than a whole heart. This happens even to well-meaning Christians today. We read a book pointing out some cool benefits of balancing our chakras and think, "That's not so bad," and we dig deeper. But whether it's unpacking nifty parallels between the Qur'an and the Bible, reading horoscopes just for fun, or allowing a sea of anti-Christian television shows to float through our heads, it's hard to know when innocent curiosity starts chipping away at rock-solid belief. The Israelites didn't just wake up one day and say, "Hey, let's abandon God." It happened bit by bit, day by day, and choice by choice.

This is why God longs for His people to not just follow Him, but to follow Him with great passion as well. He wants our desire for Him and His will to be so strong that nothing will get between His Word and us. And lest we be accused of ignoring others in our pursuit of God, remember that His Word also points us outward to direct others back to Him.

One more thing: the slaughter of the prophets at the end of the account is jarringly brutal, but it was brutally necessary. If these prophets had lived, they would have lured, over time, many Israelites back to the evil ways of a false god. This was both an affirmation of the commitment the Israelites had just made to the Lord and a preventive measure to eradicate a significant source of temptation in the future.

This passage, in no way, gives justification for modern Christians who wish to stage vigilante-style attacks on those who preach false religions. To do such a thing would be against the laws of our nation. The Israelites, however, were bound to a different set of laws. Deuteronomy had laid out for them as a people and a nation that the death penalty was proper for those who led people away from God.

Moreover, we are no longer an Old Testament people, bound only to the Law and its commands. Instead, we have the gift of the Gospel fulfilled in Christ, through whose words we may appeal to those who know nothing of Him. The slaughter of these prophets could be seen as essential for the preservation and continuation of the true faith throughout Israel. Believers needed to survive so that the Word could be passed on. The truths of God's Word in the Bible today, however, have spread across the world to such a degree that it could never be wiped out. Although we are still called to spread the Word to all those who still have not heard it, violence is not necessary to keep the faith alive.

We should, however, keep watch for false teachings within our own churches and especially within our own hearts. For such sinful beliefs, we are to have no tolerance. Repenting to the Lord from our misdeeds and evil thoughts, we receive cleansing and forgiveness.

BONUS FEATURES

Imaginary fiends: Baal and Asherah aren't the only false deities named in the Bible. The fake gods below are just a few of the others worshiped by many during Bible times.

Molech: A destroyer deity of the Ammonites referred to as an abomination; child sacrifices were made to him.

Chemosh: Called the "subduer," the chief deity of the Moabites; Jeremiah condemned the worship of Chemosh.

Dagon: The national deity of the Philistines and god of water and grain, Dagon was portrayed with the head of a human and the body of a fish; the statue of Dagon fell and broke before the ark of the covenant when the two were in the same place.

Zeus: King of the Greek gods, he's known for hurling bolts of lightning and having affairs with mortal women; in Acts 14, Barnabas is mistaken for Zeus.

Hermes: Messenger of the Greek gods, known for his winged sandals and hat, Hermes was thought to be a well-meaning trickster; in Acts 14, Paul is mistaken for Hermes.

Famous contests: We live in an age where competitions are everywhere, whether they're eating contests, reality shows, or good old sports battles. While there are countless others that have influenced history, here are two contests that stand out for their impact:

The Orteig Prize was a $25,000 reward offered in 1919 by a rich hotel owner for the first nonstop flight from New York to Paris. At least six people died in attempts to win the prize before it was claimed in 1927 by Charles Lindbergh. His flight made him a huge celebrity and set off an international craze for flying.

In the 1770s, a famine in Europe killed a large number of people. In response, the French Academie de Besancon started a search for a hearty food that could reduce the troubles associated with famine. The winner was an American import championed by Antoine Parmentier: the potato. Up to that point, many in France worried the potato might be poisonous.

CHAPTER 11

Heaven's Flamethrower

Who died: Two captains and their groups of fifty men each / King Ahaziah

How they died: Burned / sickness

Why they died: Disrespecting God and trusting another god for help

When: Circa 852 BC, during the reign of King Shalmaneser III of Assyria

Where in Scripture: 2 Kings 1

Questions. We usually think of the Bible as a book of answers. And that it is. But it's also a book full of questions. From the serpent's "Did God really say . . . ?" to Jesus' "Who do you say that I am?" questions lead the narrative of the Bible forward.

Questions are tools for teaching, but they are so often packed with emotions and, sometimes, they lack in right thinking. That's what happened with King Ahaziah. He had the right question, but he went to the wrong place for answers.

LOOKING FOR ANSWERS IN ALL THE WRONG PLACES

It's not like God's power should have been a mystery to him. Elijah alone was well enough known at this time for his dramatic confrontations, such as with the prophets of Baal, that Ahaziah should have known right off the bat exactly where to turn for help. Unfortunately, Ahaziah followed in the ways of his mother, Jezebel—who likely still whispered in his ear—and thought only of pagan gods when the going got rough.

That's too bad, because things turned downright rotten for Ahaziah shortly into his reign as king of Israel. Sensing weakness, Moab successfully rebelled against Israel, leaving the nation short the generous tribute Moab had been paying each year. Then Ahaziah fell through a window lattice in his house and injured himself very badly. He became so ill as a result that his survival was far from certain.

And if this were a happy story of repentance, that would be the point where the king prayed to God for help and received healing and forgiveness. However, that is not this story. Instead, Ahaziah sent messengers to the god of the Philistine city of Ekron: Baal-zebub.

That wasn't going to fly with God, so the angel of the Lord came to Elijah and told him to intercept the messengers and give them a new message for the king. So Elijah found the messengers and gave them God's words for the king. Wisely, the messengers turned around and went back to Ahaziah, forgetting their foolish mission to go to Ekron. Knowing the king wouldn't be happy to see them back so soon, they told him right away about the strange man they met on their way. His message, they

THAT REMINDS ME: THE NAME *BAAL-ZEBUB* SHOULD LOOK FAMILIAR. THE *BAAL* PART WAS USED TO REFER TO SEVERAL DIFFERENT DEITIES AND SIMPLY MEANT "LORD." PUT TOGETHER HERE, IT FORMS A TERM MEANING "LORD OF THE FLIES," A BITING INSULT FOR THE DEITY COMMONLY CALLED *BAAL-ZEBUL* OR "BAAL IS PRINCE."

said, was this: "Thus says the LORD, Is it because there is no God in Israel that you are sending to inquire of Baal-zebub, the god of Ekron? Therefore you shall not come down from the bed to which you have gone up, but you shall surely die" (2 Kings 1:6).

Cause and effect are laid out right there, clear as day. The message should have been enough to turn the king to repentance on the spot or, at least, to make him curl up in the fetal position in fear. Rather, he focused on the wrong thing and asked for a description of the man. They told him, and the hairy clothes and leather belt gave Elijah away. It's easy to imagine Ahaziah snarling, "Elijah. It had to be Elijah." His parents' struggles with Elijah were no mystery to him, and he'd surely heard that Elijah wasn't one for empty threats. Again, this should have caused only fear and immediate repentance. Again, though, it did not.

Ahaziah wasn't about to let Elijah feel like the boss. It was time to turn the tables, so Ahaziah sent a captain with fifty soldiers to wrangle Elijah and, perhaps, even kill him. When the soldiers arrived, Elijah was sitting on top of a hill. With little respect, the captain demanded that Elijah come down. But Elijah wasn't having it. He said, "If I am a man of God, let fire come down from heaven and consume you and your fifty" (v. 10). And just like the altar on Mount Carmel, the soldiers were devoured by fire from heaven.

> **JUST WONDERING:** IN THE PREVIOUS CHAPTER, ELIJAH WAS ON MOUNT CARMEL CONTESTING THE PROPHETS OF BAAL. ONCE AGAIN, HERE, HE'S UP HIGH, AND THIS ISN'T THE LAST TIME ELIJAH SHOWS UP ON TOP OF A HILL. BOTH ELIJAH AND MOSES LATER APPEARED WITH JESUS ON THE MOUNT OF TRANSFIGURATION. WHY DOES A HILLTOP SEEM LIKE A GOOD PLACE FOR A PROPHET TO BE? WHY DO YOU THINK SO MANY KEY BIBLE EVENTS HAPPENED ON HILLS OR MOUNTAINS?

Was this going to stop the king from getting what he wanted? No way! He sent another captain with fifty more men. This captain apparently didn't get the message about what happened to the previous crew because he was even ruder than the first captain, saying, "O man of God, this is the king's order, 'Come down quickly!'" (v. 11). Who knows why, after decades of doing otherwise, he thought Elijah would be inclined to obey a command from a wicked king. Just like the time before, Elijah called for fire, and fire from heaven incinerated the bones, flesh, and clothes of the captain and the fifty men. Mercifully, at least from the sound of it, the fire was so strong and fast that death was immediate.

The message should have gotten through to Ahaziah by now to try something else, but the king was nothing if not consistent—consistently foolish. Besides, he had plenty of men in his army. What were a hundred soldiers to a king, especially when his own death was on the line? By now, you can probably guess what happened next. The king sent another captain and another fifty soldiers to Elijah.

While we don't know if this captain served the true God before this day, he almost certainly did afterward. At the least, he was a wise man who had heard what had happened to the others. Rather than shouting demands at Elijah, he knelt at Elijah's feet and begged Elijah to spare his life and the lives of his men.

Hearing the captain and having mercy on him, the angel of the Lord told Elijah to go with the captain and to have no fear. So, at last, Elijah went to King Ahaziah. The king did not make any last effort to apologize or seek God's forgiveness from His representative, so Elijah repeated God's message from earlier: because the king sought help from a false god, he would soon die.

That is exactly what happened, and the two-year reign of Ahaziah ended, with no children to succeed him. Instead, another brother of their wicked parents, Ahab and Jezebel, took the throne.

WHY IS THIS IN THE BIBLE?

When your sink leaks, you call a plumber. When a kangaroo wanders into your yard, a zoo keeper might help. When your jump shot is way off, you ask your coach for help. And when your world is falling apart and you don't know what the future holds, there's only one place to go for help: Mom.

Just kidding. While, your mom might actually help, the best answer is God, because not only can He reassure you about the past and present, but He also knows exactly what is coming in the future. That's something no one else can do, and it was true in Ahaziah's day too. If only Ahaziah had remembered that.

While we might not call on pagan deities, we are just as guilty as Ahaziah of looking in the wrong places for help. Money, self-help books, and celebrities might seem to provide answers, but they're never the first place we should go. Although many of the solutions God provides for our troubles involve people throughout our world, we are to always go to Him first, praying for help, for comfort, and for guidance. Only then can we know that He is leading us rather than us leading us.

And that right there is the biggest danger. We live in a culture of pride and self-

THAT REMINDS ME: MANY OTHERS IN BIBLE TIMES BESIDES AHAZIAH WENT LOOKING FOR ANSWERS IN THE WRONG PLACES. NOTABLY, THE WISE MEN FIRST WENT TO JERUSALEM, BECAUSE THAT'S WHERE THEY THOUGHT A NEW KING WOULD BE BORN. WHILE THEY WERE WRONG, THEY DID AT LEAST GET THE CLUE THEY NEEDED FROM GOD'S WORD. THUS, THEY WENT TO BETHLEHEM TO WORSHIP THE ONE WHO ANSWERS EVERY NEED WE HAVE.

sufficiency. Admitting that anyone, even God, knows more than we do about what's best for us is difficult. Pride, which turns us into our own gods, pulls us just as far from God's will as Ahaziah ever was. That's why constant connection with God, praying at all times for all needs both large and small, is essential. It keeps us dependent on the only One who is eternally dependable.

Also, like that final captain, we are to humble ourselves before God and honor those who bring His Word. Our pastors, teachers, and parents are in our lives to guide us along God's righteous path to heaven. Showing respect for them is never an option but is always essential.

BONUS FEATURES

Miracle man: Keeping in mind that every miracle credited to Elijah is really a miracle done by God, Elijah built an amazing résumé of miraculous moments, unmatched by anyone in the Old Testament since the time of Moses.

Elijah's Top-Ten List of Miraculous Moments

1. Initiated a three-year drought
2. Was fed bread and meat twice a day by ravens for a time
3. Enjoyed a bottomless jar of flour and jug of oil while staying with a widow
4. Raised the widow's son from the dead
5. Won a contest against 450 prophets of Baal
6. Ran faster than Ahab's chariot over a long distance
7. After witnessing a mighty wind, an earthquake, and a fire, he heard the Lord speak in a whisper
8. Witnessed the frying of one hundred of Ahaziah's soldiers
9. Parted the Jordan River with his cloak
10. Went up to heaven in a fiery chariot

Starting a fire: Never start a fire without your parents' permission, so get that first. That said, once you've gathered together your wood, bark, paper, coals, or whatever you're planning to burn, you're going to need something to light them with. So the next time you're stuck on an island or in the woods and need a way to keep warm, boil water, cook food, or frighten animals, try one or more of these tools to get the fire started:

- Waterproof matches
- A lighter
- A pop can and toothpaste or chocolate (for polishing the can)
- Steel wool and a 9-volt battery
- A magnifying lens or glasses
- A shoelace and flexible branch
- A flint and steel
- A round balloon filled with water
- Something that's already on fire

CHAPTER 12

PUPPY CHOW

Who died: Jezebel

How she died: Thrown out a window and eaten by dogs

Why she died: Wickedness

When: 841 BC, which is also the earliest firmly documented date in Chinese history and the beginning of the Gonghe Regency

Where in Scripture: 2 Kings 9

At the top of the heap of wicked women in the Bible, Jezebel sits supreme. A powerful queen who pushed her husband and her nation around, Jezebel had everything a girl could want. But that wasn't nearly enough for her. She always needed more, and she was willing to do anything to get it.

Take in this partial list of Jezebel's evil acts:

1. Sheltered and fed pagan priests, while promoting false gods
2. Ordered the deaths of many of God's prophets and sought to destroy worship of the one true God
3. Threatened Elijah's life
4. Had a man killed to get his vineyard for her husband

In short, if only she were a little less R-rated, she would make a great evil queen for a Disney movie. Jezebel had nastiness running through her veins. Considering that, it's no wonder her ending was tasteless and demeaning as she went to the dogs, literally—and we're not talking about cuddly dalmatians.

A HISTORY OF HATE

As tempting as it is to jump right to her grizzly end, Jezebel accumulated too "impressive" of a résumé to overlook. In fact, her very own actions are what set the stage for her demise. The section with Elijah and the prophets of Baal touched on Jezebel's support of pagan priests, and 1 Kings 18:4 references her attempts to kill the Lord's prophets.

In her defense, Jezebel was a foreigner, the daughter of the Phoenician king, and hadn't been raised in the fear and knowledge of God. Nevertheless, she wasted no time importing her own religion and doing everything in her power to obliterate the worship of Israel's God. She couldn't care less about their history and the legacy of protection and promises made between Israel and God. Jezebel wanted things her way, and she wanted them yesterday. Fortunately for her, her weak-willed hubby, Ahab, was only too happy to oblige.

To see how fearsome she was, we need only to go to the aftermath of God's victory against the prophets of Baal. Elijah had seen and performed numerous miracles, including raising the dead, and he'd just defeated and killed hundreds of Jezebel's pet prophets at Mount Carmel. During all this, he had no trouble speaking directly to King Ahab, mocking Baal's prophets, and reprimanding all the people of Israel. But then, Jezebel heard what happened and sent Elijah a death threat. Suddenly, the bold prophet was terrified and ran off into the wilderness to die. (Spoiler alert: he didn't die.) But that's how scary Jezebel was. No one wanted to mess with her.

And all that was before the events of Naboth's vineyard.

EARNING THE GRAPES OF WRATH

One day, King Ahab looked out his window at a great piece of land used for a vineyard and had a super idea for where to plant his new vegetable garden. So, Ahab asked the vineyard's owner, a man named Naboth, to trade him the vineyard for an even better one the king had elsewhere; or, better yet, for good old money. While trying to be polite, Naboth said, "No way."

PUPPY CHOW 125

He knew that Israelite law at the time meant that his land had been passed down through his family for generations before him and would be passed to his descendants for generations afterward. It wasn't just land to him. It was his family's legacy from the Lord. Also, according to the law, no one could take it away from him.

Old Ahab knew all this, but he still wanted it, so he went home and pouted, refusing to eat his supper. It didn't take Jezebel long to find out what had happened. Ahab stuck out his lip and told her something like, "The big meanie wouldn't give me his vineyard." That wasn't going to cut it with Jezebel, and, for all her shortcomings, she was, at the least, a supportive wife. She told Ahab, "You are still king. Eat and be happy. I'll take care of the vineyard." Picture Ahab's big, goofy grin as his wife began plotting.

Since evil scheming came naturally to her, it didn't take long for her to set her plan in motion. Jezebel sent letters to everyone important in Naboth's community and instructed them to find a couple of guys to accuse Naboth publicly of cursing God and the king (not that Jezebel would ever curse God herself). Then they were to find Naboth guilty of the fake crime and stone him. Everyone—including people Naboth had known his whole life—was so terrified of the king

THAT REMINDS ME: AS A RESULT OF THESE EVENTS, GOD HAD ELIJAH CURSE AHAB THAT WHEN HE DIED, HE WOULD HAVE HIS BLOOD LICKED UP BY DOGS IN THE SAME PLACE THAT NABOTH DIED (1 KINGS 21). ADDITIONALLY, DOGS WOULD EAT JEZEBEL, AND ALL OF AHAB'S MALE DESCENDANTS WOULD DIE SOON AFTER.

and queen that they did exactly as instructed. Jezebel heard the happy news, and sent Ahab to claim the land as his own, without spending a cent.

Ahab died a few years after the vineyard takeover when he was shot with an arrow during battle. He bled out all over his chariot, and his blood was lapped up by nearby dogs. From that point on, Jezebel continued to sow corruption through the reigns of two of her sons.

DELICIOUS, DISGUSTING DOGGY DINNER

It was during the reign of Jezebel's son, Joram, that the bell finally tolled for Jez. As a result of Joram not surprisingly following in the wicked ways of his mom and dad, God had Elijah's successor, Elisha, send one of his servants to proclaim Jehu as king in Joram's place. Jehu wasn't just a nobody; he was the commander of Joram's own army. Because of this, it was especially bad news for Joram that God also commissioned Jehu to kill Joram, as well as his ally, King Ahaziah of Judah. Even more severe, Jehu was to cut off the line of Ahab completely, killing all his male descendants.

JUST WONDERING: YOU MAY ALREADY BE REMEMBERING HOW DAVID WAS ANOINTED AS THE FUTURE KING EVEN WHILE SAUL HELD THE THRONE. WHY WOULD GOD DO THIS IN BOTH THESE ACCOUNTS? WHY IN SOME CASES IN THE OLD TESTAMENT WAS VIOLENCE THE RECOMMENDED SOLUTION AND OTHER TIMES MERCY WAS PRAISED?

Jehu, who was known for his wild chariot driving, took up his assignment eagerly. He blazed toward the kings in his chariot, shot Joram through the heart with an arrow, and had his men shoot a fleeing Ahaziah as well. Then, it was on to Jezebel.

When word of what Jehu had done reached the wily old queen, she sought her weapons and prepared for his coming. Her weapons, of course, were her jewels and makeup, the tools of seduction and power she had used against men her whole life. She looked out the window, appearing every bit the monarch, as Jehu arrived outside. But she knew the score, and she wasn't about to beg and plead to change his mind. No, Jezebel wanted to go out on her own terms, so she sneered instead, "Is it peace, you Zimri, murderer of your master?" (2 Kings 9:31).

THAT REMINDS ME: JEZEBEL'S FINAL WORDS ARE AN UNVEILED TAUNT AT JEHU, AN ATTEMPT TO PLANT DOUBT IN HIS MIND ABOUT HIS FUTURE AS KING. ZIMRI WAS A CAVALRY COMMANDER WHO HAD ASSASSINATED KING ELAH OF ISRAEL DECADES EARLIER. THIS WAS DONE BECAUSE OF THE EVIL OF HIS FATHER AND HIS FAMILY. JEZEBEL'S POINT, HOWEVER, IS THAT ZIMRI REIGNED AS KING A MERE SEVEN DAYS BEFORE BEING ATTACKED AND DYING IN A FIRE.

Jehu was wise enough not to get in a war of words with an opponent as slippery as Jezebel. Instead, he called up through Jezebel's window to the servants inside with her, "Who is on my side?" (v. 32). A few of her servants basically nodded out the window to him, so he commanded them to throw her out. A moment later, the incomparable Jezebel went flying out the window and landed on the ground. Her blood splattered on the wall and the horses, who then trampled her.

Jehu could have dealt with the mess right away. Leaving dead queens in the street wasn't exactly good manners. But wouldn't you know, good old Jehu and his men were hungry from a long day of slaughtering rulers, so Jehu headed inside to drink and chow down. If God wanted a king without a weak stomach, Jehu was definitely the right guy. And just to show some respect for the dead, he commanded his soldiers to bury Jezebel, since she was a queen and the daughter of a king and all that. Apparently, Jehu had forgotten God's warning that no one would bury Jezebel.

Alas, Jezebel wouldn't have the privilege of a burial. After looking outside, Jehu's men came back to him to report that only her skull and feet and the palms of her hands were left. The neighborhood dogs had gobbled up all the rest. So, in the end, both Jehu and the canines were well fed.

Just to wrap things up in a delightful fashion, here are the final verses from 2 Kings 9: "In the territory of Jezreel the dogs shall eat the flesh of Jezebel, and the corpse of Jezebel shall be as dung on the face of the field in the territory of Jezreel, so that no one can say, This is Jezebel" (vv. 36–37). There would be no tombstone, no grave, no monument to her life or her death, and soon all her sons would follow her into death.

THAT REMINDS ME: NOW, AS ALWAYS, JEZEBEL IS TIED TO HER NEMESIS, THE PROPHET ELIJAH, IN THAT NEITHER OF THEM IS BURIED. THAT IS, OBVIOUSLY, WHERE THE SIMILARITY STOPS. FOR, AS SHE WAS DENIED HONOR AT THE END OF HER LIFE, HE WAS GIVEN THE ULTIMATE HONOR IN BEING TAKEN ALIVE INTO HEAVEN IN A FIERY CHARIOT.

WHY IS THIS IN THE BIBLE?

It's crazy to think that anyone could actually deserve to be thrown out a window and eaten by dogs, but if anyone had it coming, Jezebel did. Beyond the despicable deeds recorded in Scripture, without a doubt the full list of her evil acts could fill a phone book.

However, even though we're not usually as blatant about it, you could say the same thing for each and every one of us. Sins accumulate daily by the dozens and hundreds through idle thoughts, biting words, and ill-considered actions. As soon as we start thinking we're making it through the day without sin, we're clobbered over the head with our horrid pride. Our sins are so many and would take so long to count, it's an unmatched blessing that God has forgiven each and every one already.

While Jehu is a model of following God's will in eliminating evil influences, Jezebel is still the central character here, and there's not much room for hope in her story. She lived under the Law, and, as such, her story doesn't show us where to go.

Although her husband, Ahab, actually repented of his sin before the end of his life, Jezebel, by all appearances, never did. In that, she stands as an icon of what willful unrepentance looks like. She rejected everyone and everything that had anything to do with the true God. As far as she was concerned, none of His gifts were real or for her, and she was not about to seek them, no matter what the cost of her denial.

Jezebel, her life and her death, should terrify us into never wanting to repeat her mistakes or her fate—the earthly one or the eternal one reserved for unrepentant sinners. All we can do when looking at a wholly evil person such as her is thank God for working in us through His Gospel to show us His love, His Son, and His forgiveness. How greatly we need God's mercy and the great gift of repentant hearts that seek only His will and not our own.

BONUS FEATURES

Unsavory Scripture suppers: From John the Baptist's locusts to some of the foods that were okayed for the Old Testament Israelites, the Bible mentions many meals that would turn our stomachs. Here are a few of the least appetizing:

Gagging on gold: In Exodus 32:19–20, Moses was furious that the Israelites made and worshiped a golden calf while he was getting the Ten Commandments from God. Proving that a mad Moses made no one happy, he ground the calf into gold dust, mixed it with water, and forced the people to drink it.

Been there, dung that: Not long after Ezekiel ate a scroll that happened to taste like honey, God commanded Ezekiel (Ezekiel 4:10–17) to eat bread baked directly on top of cow poop. And that's only because God relented from His original plan to have Ezekiel use people droppings instead.

Baby bites: In 2 Kings 6:25–30, Samaria was under siege and food was scarce. As awful as things were, there was no excuse for these two women who ate the baby of one mother and then fought when the second mother changed her mind about sharing her own child for a meal.

Good flavor, but a horrible aftertaste: The fruit in Genesis 3 looked absolutely delicious and would make Eve wise like God, so she chowed down on it and even gave some to her husband. That's when the taste turned really bitter as sin entered the world. As a result of those bites, we would taste death.

Extreme earthly eats: The Bible is not the only place to find meals that few find flavorful.

Scotland: In a meal called haggis, the liver, lungs, and heart of a sheep are ground up and served.

Cambodia: If you like your food with legs, try a-ping, a type of tarantula fried and served on a stick.

Vietnam and the Philippines: Balut is a soft-boiled, fertilized duck embryo, still in the shell, so the duck parts are quite visible.

CHAPTER 13

CAUSING AN UPROAR

Who died: King Darius's advisers and their families

How they died: Broken to pieces by lions

Why they died: Scheming for power

When: 539 BC, five years after the birth of Sun Tzu, military genius and author of *The Art of War*

Where in Scripture: Daniel 6

There are many ways of trying to make a living by being clever. You could be a scientist, a comedian, an engineer, or choose any other profession where planning and smarts go hand in hand.

There are even ways to earn money being tricky. You could be a dog trainer, a magician, or a con artist. Okay, maybe the last one isn't such a good idea. Something else that isn't a good idea? Trying to outsmart God. No matter how clever you are, it just isn't going to work—ever!

Unfortunately, some people only learn that lesson the hard way. If only the clever guys who schemed against Daniel had discovered that earlier, their ending might have been a little less grisly.

OH, DANNY BOY

Everyone remembers Daniel, mostly for the story of the lions' den, but there was a lot more to him than that. As a youth, he was taken prisoner by the Babylonians, dragged away from Judah, and relocated in Nebuchadnezzar's palace. Young people of noble stock, such as Daniel, could become useful servants to the king in years to come if they did what they were told.

But, while Daniel wasn't rebellious, he felt it wasn't right for him to eat the king's rich food, which was likely unclean according to God's commands. So he convinced the chief eunuch to let him and his friends Shadrach, Meshach, and Abednego eat yummy veggies instead. And wouldn't you know it, they grew healthier and stronger than any of the young folks eating the king's fancy food. Before long, Daniel and his friends were recognized for their wisdom by the king, and then another of Daniel's skills showed up.

THAT REMINDS ME: YOU LIKELY RECOGNIZE DANIEL'S FRIENDS AS THE THREE MEN IN THE FIERY FURNACE. ONE INTERESTING FACT WITH THESE FOUR IS THAT THEY ALL HAD BOTH HEBREW NAMES (FROM BIRTH) AND BABYLONIAN NAMES (ASSIGNED WHEN THEY WERE CAPTURED). DANIEL IS KNOWN TO US BY HIS HEBREW NAME, RATHER THAN BELTASHAZZAR, HIS BABYLONIAN NAME. HOWEVER, THE OTHER THREE ARE KNOWN TO US MAINLY BY THEIR BABYLONIAN NAMES.

Twice, King Nebuchadnezzar had dreams that no one could interpret until Daniel explained the dreams according to what God had shown him. After he interpreted the first dream, Daniel was made ruler over Babylon and all its wise men. And even though the second dream was a proclamation that Nebuchadnezzar would go crazy and run wild like an animal for months, Daniel received no punishment.

After that, more than thirty years went by until Scripture mentions Daniel again. By then, Daniel was an old man in his eighties and Nebuchadnezzar's son was king. While Daniel still served the king, he no longer held much power and had been largely forgotten. However, during one of the king's parties, a supernatural hand wrote mysterious words on a wall in front of the king and his guests. It was the perfect time for Daniel to reappear, so he did, explaining that the message from God said the king would die and have his kingdom stripped away. Again, though, his wisdom was so clear that even these dire words against the king resulted in Daniel being promoted to third in charge of the kingdom. That very night, the king was killed and King Darius became the new ruler.

Although an old man, Daniel remained prominent. It didn't matter that he was a foreigner, an outsider. His advice was so good that he was named one of the top-three officials and soon was outshining them all. Great news, huh? If your name was Daniel, it was. As for the king's other advisers, they thought it was time to take him down.

THE GRAND SCHEME

King Darius was so pleased with Daniel that he was planning to put him in charge of the whole kingdom, second in command after only the king himself. That's a crazy amount of power for one man who wasn't even from around there—at least that's what the other advisers and wise men thought. Tired of waiting for Daniel to mess up, the wise guys let their inner mudslingers out and went digging for something, anything they could use to mar his name. There was, as they quickly realized, no dirt to find, which meant it was up to them to invent some.

THAT REMINDS ME: DANIEL AND JOSEPH (JACOB'S SON) ARE PARALLEL FIGURES IN ISRAELITE HISTORY. BOTH WERE TAKEN AGAINST THEIR WILL INTO ANOTHER COUNTRY, GOING FROM POSITIONS OF PRIVILEGE TO SERVANTHOOD. FROM THERE, BOTH WERE TAKEN BEFORE KINGS WHO NEEDED SOMEONE TO INTERPRET THEIR DREAMS AND TELL THE FUTURE OF THEIR KINGDOMS, AND BOTH WERE APPOINTED TO HIGH-RANKING POSITIONS IN THE KINGDOMS.

It didn't take them long to figure out Daniel's "weakness": his faithfulness to God. These presidents and satraps—fancy words for the powerful advisers and officials—sneaked in to see King Darius when Daniel wasn't around. They told him that the three presidents and the 120 satraps—regional officials—had all agreed on a great new plan. Darius should have been suspicious. Besides the fact that Daniel, one of the presidents, wasn't present, it would have been highly unlikely for them to have received opinions from all 120 satraps, who were spread out throughout the whole kingdom. It's not like they could send email or schedule a conference call.

But Darius didn't stop them. They had, after all, begun with the most important words: "O King Darius, live forever!" (Daniel 6:6). But that was just the start of the flattery. The rest of their presentation was pure ego stroking. Their great king was awesome! The best ever! And he should be treated like a god. So, they proposed that for the next thirty days, no one in the kingdom could pray to any other god or man, but could pray only to King Darius. To make the law serious enough, they added that anyone who disobeyed would be thrown to the lions. And just to make sure it stuck, and that Daniel didn't find a way to wheedle out from under it, they suggested it be a full

JUST WONDERING: ORDINANCES PUT IN PLACE ACCORDING TO "THE LAW OF THE MEDES AND THE PERSIANS" (DANIEL 6:8; SEE ALSO ESTHER 1:19) COULD NOT BE CHANGED, EVEN BY THE KING. HOW WOULD YOUR DECISION-MAKING BE DIFFERENT IF YOUR DECISIONS WERE UNDER THE SAME CONSTRAINT? WHAT IF ONCE YOU PICKED A FRIEND, AN AFTER-SCHOOL ACTIVITY, OR A JOB, YOU COULD NEVER CHANGE IT?

and proper law that could not be canceled or changed.

Darius eagerly signed on. He was king. Who wouldn't want to pray to him? It likely never occurred to him that any of his subjects would even think of missing out on this chance to show their ruler how much they loved him. It occurred to the officials though.

As soon as Daniel heard that the law was in force, he got on his knees and prayed to God. He did exactly as he'd always done. Law or no law, only one God would receive Daniel's prayers, and it wasn't the king.

Daniel just happened to be praying near an open window. And the schemers just happened to be outside that window, watching him. They were pleased with themselves as they watched Daniel pray exactly as they'd known he would. Evidence in hand, they went to the king, asked him if he remembered the law—a truly manipulative question designed to make the king reaffirm the law. Then, they mentioned that Daniel, one of the exiles from Judah, ignored the king and the law by praying to his God. Notice that they didn't call Daniel the king's adviser or the second-in-command or anything like that. They wanted to make it clear that he was an outsider who cared nothing about their people's laws.

The advisers thought the king would be furious with Daniel about this, but they were sadly mistaken. The king was upset, but not at Daniel. Rather, he spent the rest of the day trying to find a loophole in his law so he wouldn't have to enforce the punishment. "Not happening," the advisers reminded him, behind their barely concealed grins.

RIP-ROARING FUN IN THE DEN

Reluctantly, the king gave in and commanded Daniel to be thrown into the den of lions when the sun went down. Still hoping, but not really believing, the king said to Daniel, "May your God, whom you serve continually, deliver you!" (Daniel 6:16). The king truly cared about and valued old man Daniel, but he knew there was no chance Daniel would survive the night.

A stone with the king's seal on it was placed in the opening of the den, guaranteeing there would be no help from the outside. Darius went back to his palace so distraught that he didn't eat or sleep or accept any form of entertainment.

Try to picture Daniel in that den. Did he stare the lions down or cuddle up next to one? Was he fearful, apprehensive, at peace? Did he expect to die for his faith or to be saved like his friends in the fiery furnace? One thing is certain. Daniel did the very thing he'd been thrown into the lions' den for in the first place: he prayed. It's great storytelling that the text doesn't tell us what happened next, that it doesn't say a word about what happened to Daniel from the moment the den was sealed until the king returned the next morning.

> **THAT REMINDS ME:** JAMES 5:16 SAYS, "THE PRAYER OF A RIGHTEOUS PERSON HAS GREAT POWER AS IT IS WORKING."

Nearing the den, exhausted and grieving, the king called out to Daniel, not expecting a response: "O Daniel, servant of the living God, has your God, whom you serve continually, been able to deliver you from the lions?" (v. 20). Darius must have shaken in shock when Daniel's voice shouted from the den, "O king, live forever!" (v. 21). Daniel went on to explain how God's angel shut the lions' hungry jaws—and restrained their claws as well—because Daniel had not sinned in this matter against either God or the king.

Darius was absolutely delighted as his servants helped Daniel, completely unharmed, out of the den. And that is when the scheming turned on the schemers. Daniel had passed the trial by lion, and Darius knew exactly why these evil men had set up the whole thing. So, as punishment, they would receive the same fate they had planned for Daniel. The schemers and their wives and children were all thrown into the lions' den.

And if the thought of lions sinking their teeth into your flesh and tearing into you with their claws gives you the creeps, keep reading. The lions not only mauled their new victims, but also attacked so ferociously that they broke the people's bones into pieces before they reached the floor of the den. That's blood and bone marrow and vital organs spilling out all over the place. These were not pretty deaths, but they were mercifully quickly carried out.

No pun intended, but including the wives and children as well seems like overkill to our modern minds. Remember, however, that the killing of the men's families here was not God's idea; it was Darius's. Likely, he did it as a warning to anyone in the future who would put personal ambitions and grievances above the good of the kingdom and the king.

So impressed was Darius with how Daniel's God protected him that he made a decree that all people in the kingdom were to fear and respect the wonder-working God of Daniel. Daniel's faith led to an amazing proclamation in honor of God. This did not mean that Darius suddenly became a faithful believer in the true God. He still reigned in a kingdom that believed in numerous gods. He simply believed that Daniel's God deserved a position of high respect. And God would surely bring good out of such a proclamation.

WHY IS THIS IN THE BIBLE?

Scottish novelist and poet Sir Walter Scott wrote, "Oh! What a tangled web we weave when first we practice to deceive." For certain, that is one of the lessons of this account. The king's scheming officials and advisers weren't forced into attacking Daniel. Here are other options they could have chosen to benefit themselves and the kingdom.

1. Show appreciation for Daniel and the good advice he gave the king, which made the kingdom better and stronger.
2. Ask Daniel for advice on how to be wiser themselves.

3. Work hard to become better officials and advisers with the hope of eventually surpassing Daniel.

4. Wait for Daniel to die of natural causes. He was in his eighties, which was very old for that time period.

Although none of us is likely to ever put together a scheme as treacherous as Daniel's enemies, it's a rare person who doesn't at some point make plans to get even with someone else, to trick them, or to get an unfair advantage. This story especially warns us not to attack the reputations of people who are engaged in godly pursuits. Other students, teachers, pastors, and teammates should not be seen as opponents to work around, plot against, or manipulate.

The second and most important lesson from this account is that God will always hear the prayers of His people and answer in the way that He decides is appropriate. It doesn't mean that the dangers and burdens in our lives will be removed completely. Daniel was still thrown in the lions' den. It doesn't even mean our lives will be spared, for even if Daniel had died, God would have still gathered him to his eternal, heavenly home. But knowing that God hears and answers our prayers should make us excited to continue praying to Him about everything we need.

There is no earthly obstacle so great it should be able to separate us from our desire to talk to God. There is no threat worse than separation from God—which some call hell—so why would we ever separate ourselves from doing what God has commanded?

One last thought: a hero of the faith as a young man and in his old age, Daniel is a great picture of what a life of faith can look like. It's not our strength, our wisdom, our experience, or our potential that matters to God. God cares only about being the Lord of our lives and the caretaker of our hearts as we receive and treasure the gift of faith.

BONUS FEATURES

Good plans gone bad or bad plans gone good: The Bible records a great supply of these, not the least of which is the devil's plan to have Christ killed. Boy, did that ever backfire on him. Read on for two more big plans that blew up in their planners' faces:

Balak and Balaam: During the time the children of Israel were making their journey to the Promised Land, they were also building a mighty reputation as a military force. For this reason, Balak, king of Moab, hired the mysterious soothsayer Balaam to speak prophetic curses against Israel in hopes of weakening them. After an ordeal with an angel and a talking donkey, Balaam was convinced to do what God wanted, so each of the four times he was supposed to speak curses, he spoke instead God's words of prophetic blessing upon Israel and doom upon its enemies, including Moab.

Haman: Promoted to a position of power by Ahasuerus, the king of Persia, Haman let a personal slight by Mordecai the Jew turn into a hateful desire to destroy all Jews. To this end, he approached the king and described the Jews as an enemy living among them. Haman proposed a bribe if the king would let him take care of these "traitors." But when Mordecai and his niece, Queen Esther—who was a Jew in secret—discovered the plan, Esther risked her life to reveal it. Thanks to her faithfulness, the Jews were saved, and Haman's schemes were exposed. In the end, the gallows that Haman had built to hang Mordecai on was used to hang Haman himself.

I ain't lion!: Lions are featured prominently in art, literature, and symbols of family and national identity. Appearances in classic literature include these:

"Androcles and the Lion": Aesop's version of this story shares how an escaped slave, Androcles, meets an upset lion, pulls a thorn from its paw, and becomes friends with it. Several years later, Androcles is recaptured by the Romans and thrown into a stadium to be killed by wild

lions. The same lion is sent to ravage him, recognizes his friend, and is affectionate toward Androcles, resulting in both lion and man being set free.

The Nemean lion: The lion killed by Hercules in his first labor was a man-eater; its skin, which Hercules later wore, was invulnerable.

"The Lion and the Mouse": In another of Aesop's fables, a mouse begs for freedom from a lion who had captured him; later, when the lion is captured by hunters, the mouse chews through the net and frees the lion as a way to say thanks.

The Cowardly Lion: Although a friend to Dorothy, the Tin Man, and the Scarecrow, this lion is terrified of pretty much everything else.

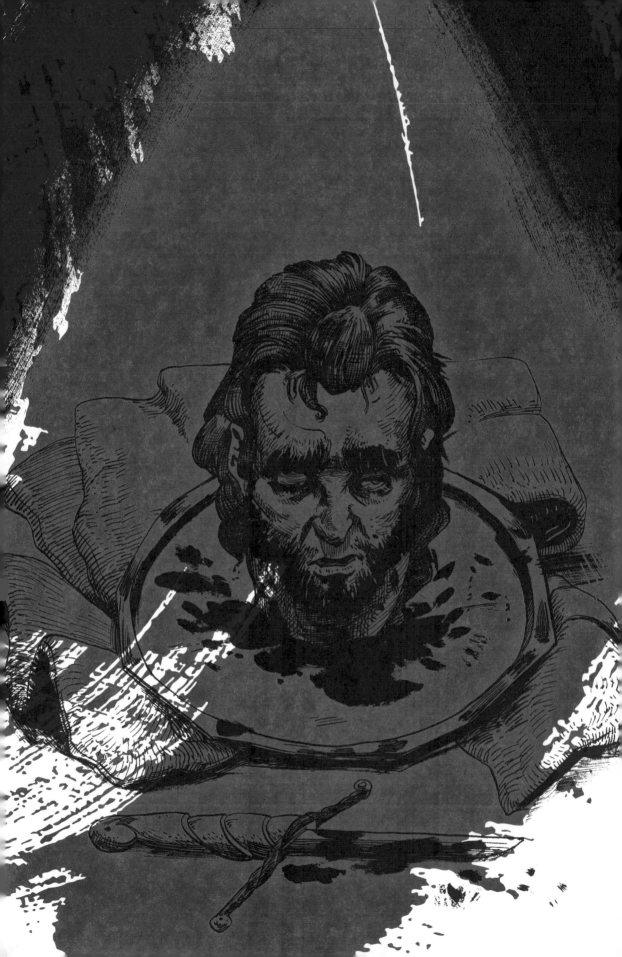

CHAPTER 14

DECAPITATION DANCE

Who died: John the Baptist

How he died: Beheading

Why he died: Herod's human weakness and John's faithful preaching

When: AD 31 or 32, around the time that Marcus Otho, future Roman emperor, was born

Where in Scripture: Matthew 14:1–12 (also Mark 6:14–29)

By and large, wild men are not good role models. No mother sees her baby boy and says, "Wow! Wouldn't it be great if he became a misunderstood, bug-eating hermit." Nor does she say, "And I hope he grows up to be way less important than his cousin, makes lots of important people mad, and dies an unjust, early death."

Yeah, for some reason, none of those sentiments appear on new baby greeting cards or in the midst of lullabies. Think about your own goals and ambitions. While lots of people listened to John, and he was clearly a celebrity, there weren't really any other perks to his job. Would you be willing to live the kind of life John the Baptist did just to serve God?

Besides the isolation and gross food, John dressed himself like a prophet of old, which was not exactly asking people to treat him nicely. For the most part, prophets were mocked, persecuted, beaten, disrespected, and killed. While being God's prophet sounds awesome, dressing like one was the equivalent of wearing a neon "Kick Me" sign. A prophet's life could be rewarding, but it was never going to be easy.

THAT REMINDS ME: JOHN THE BAPTIST IS FOREVER LINKED WITH THE PROPHET ELIJAH BECAUSE OF PASSAGES LIKE MALACHI 4:5–6, WHICH PROPHESIED THE RETURN OF ONE LIKE ELIJAH TO PREPARE THE WAY FOR THE LORD. THIS PASSAGE COMES RIGHT AT THE END OF THE OLD TESTAMENT, BRIDGING THE OLD AND THE NEW, MUCH LIKE JOHN DID IN CONNECTING THE PROPHETS OF THE PAST WITH THE COMING MESSIAH.

FROM A MIRACLE BABY TO A MIRACULOUS WASHING

Four Gospels present four different introductions of John the Baptist. Not that they conflict, but they each come at John from different viewpoints that flesh out the man, his purpose, and God's work through him.

Matthew begins with a firm grounding in the past as Jesus' ancestry is laid bare. It dances then between recalling Old Testament prophecies and showing the fulfillment of those prophecies through the events of Christ's conception, birth, flight to Egypt, and escape from Herod's killing of the male children in Bethlehem. The message is clear that everything that is happening and about to happen is a fulfillment of God's plan, even the detail of Jesus' return to Nazareth. It's only in the context of Christ as the fulfiller of prophecy that Matthew introduces John as a man walking in the wilderness preaching repentance. And, of course, John's doing so in fulfillment of yet another prophecy.

In Mark, however, John bursts onto the scene right away. There's no account of Jesus' birth or any of that. Instead, John's presence is prophesied and John simply "appeared, baptizing in the wilderness and proclaiming a baptism of repentance for the forgiveness of sins" (Mark 1:4). It's like he materialized out of nowhere but was instantly transcendent, taking charge and making things happen.

Luke is the most detailed, orderly, and leisurely, taking its time to share insights into John's background that the others didn't find to be essential. The story in Luke cuts back and forth between John and Jesus for several chapters, weaving their stories together until one, Jesus', takes over.

It's in Luke that an angel predicted John's birth to Zechariah in the temple. It's recorded here that old Zechariah was unable to speak for months on end while his elderly wife grew larger and larger with the child inside her. It's here that John leapt in his mother's womb at the approach of his unborn cousin, Jesus, and it's here that John's birth arrived, bringing with it the return of his father's voice in a prophecy of what John's life would bring. In Luke's Gospel, John is no mystery man when he shows up in the wilderness and then baptizes Jesus. He's family.

The Book of John, named after the apostle, begins with poetry that mentions John the Baptist but makes it very clear who the focus of the text is going to be. This Gospel makes it abundantly obvious what role Christ and John each have, who they are, and who they are not.

This is just one example of the beauty of Scripture and, especially, of the Gospels. There is only one true story, but there are numerous ways to tell it. Real history always contains layers too plentiful to include them all.

JUST WONDERING: IN WHAT WAYS WOULD THE NEW TESTAMENT BE EASIER TO UNDERSTAND IF THERE WAS ONLY ONE GOSPEL BOOK INSTEAD OF FOUR? WHAT MIGHT WE MISS IN SUCH AN ARRANGEMENT? WHY DO YOU THINK GOD CHOSE TO INSPIRE MULTIPLE—SOMETIMES SEEMINGLY CONFLICTING—ACCOUNTS OF JESUS' LIFE, DEATH, AND RESURRECTION?

There is, however, one crucial account that three of the Gospels discuss and which must be highlighted in any history of John: Jesus' Baptism. With John preaching to sinners that they should be baptized with water for repentance, it must have been mystifying to him to have Jesus, the sinless Lamb of God, come to him to be baptized. He didn't process right away that Jesus wasn't being baptized for His own sake, but for ours, to tie His life and His death to our lives and our deaths. Through His humble submission to bear our sin, we would receive the benefits of true repentance and avoid the eternal death we were destined for. Perhaps John realized what was really going on when the voice of God the Father spoke and the Holy Spirit appeared as a dove.

More could be said about this and about other words from and about John, but it's time to quit putting off the inevitable. John had done his job, and his death was waiting not far down the road.

JUST WONDERING: JOHN'S ENTIRE LIFE WAS SPENT PREPARING FOR HIS PROCLAMATION OF A BAPTISM OF REPENTANCE AND OF THE COMING MESSIAH. AFTER ALL THE WAITING, HOW DO YOU THINK JOHN FELT WHEN HE SAW THE HEAVENS OPEN AND THE HOLY SPIRIT DESCEND AND HEARD THE FATHER'S VOICE DECLARE JESUS HIS BELOVED SON? WAS HE EXCITED, RELIEVED, CONFUSED, OR VINDICATED?

HOW TO GET "A HEAD" AT PARTIES

It's fun to have a talent you can show off at parties. Whether it's a dazzling wit, a stellar singing voice, or the ability to fold delicate origami figures out of napkins, you never know whom you might impress or what prize you might receive. For Herod's niece/step-daughter/grandniece, her tidy prize for her dancing talent was the promise of up to half of Herod's kingdom.

That's a crazy big reward for a dance, but none of the Herod family was especially known for wisdom.

Stepping back a bit in time, it's important to know that Herod had arrested John the Baptist for publicly condemning Herod's appalling morals. John didn't exactly congratulate Herod on his marriage to his half-brother's wife, Herodias, who herself happened to be Herod's niece. Herodias was furious about John's public words, which left Herod "no choice" but to silence John by locking him up.

Sometime later, Herod was having a good old birthday bash with his friends when who should step up as entertainment but his wife's daughter, who, as mentioned, was related to Herod in at least three different ways. She, it seemed, was a stunning—and likely provocative—dancer. Herod, who'd surely had at least a few glasses of wine, was overly impressed. Thus, his promise to give her half his kingdom. The sly girl consulted with her mother for a moment before announcing her choice for a prize: John the Baptist's head on a platter. Why not? The head of a prophet on a shiny tray makes the perfect party favor.

Obviously, Herodias didn't think prison was a severe enough punishment for John. She was going to make sure he was silenced once and for all. Promptly, the executioner chopped John's head off and his body fell to the floor. John's dis-

JUST WONDERING: WHY WOULD HEROD MAKE SUCH A FOOLISH OFFER? ONCE HE HEARD THE REQUEST, COULD HE HAVE GOTTEN OUT OF IT—ALBEIT WITH A LITTLE EMBARRASSMENT? IF SHE HAD ACTUALLY REQUESTED HALF OF HIS KINGDOM, WOULD HE HAVE GIVEN IT, OR WOULD THAT HAVE BEEN ENOUGH MOTIVATION FOR HIM TO SNEAK OUT OF THE DEAL?

ciples buried the body and then told Jesus about it. John's head, of course, was taken directly to the young dancer, who gladly presented it to her mother.

All of this is probably why Herod freaked out when he later heard about the miracles of Jesus and became convinced that Jesus was John the Baptist raised from the dead.

WHY IS THIS IN THE BIBLE?

There's no way this account could have been left out. John the Baptist was the forerunner of Christ, the prophet who preached His coming, and the man who humbly baptized his Savior. John died because he wouldn't keep quiet about what God's Word said. That's exactly the kind of outspoken vigor we should demand from our preachers, and it's the type of determination every Christian should aspire to.

It seems unfair that John should die so young, that he shouldn't even get the chance to see Jesus complete His mission of dying and rising from the dead for the sins of the world. Imagine how much John would have enjoyed proclaiming Christ's resurrection after the fact! Instead, he preceded his cousin in death. His work was done, and his heavenly reward awaited him.

This story could be taken to mean that Christians are simply at the whims of powerful unbelievers who could harm and even end our lives at a moment's notice. And while long earthly lives are not promised to us, that is not the message here. Yes, we do not know what the future holds for any of us. No, having a strong faith and serving God well does not earn us a "Get Out of Jail and Suffering" card.

God can and will call us to Him at a time and place of His choosing, not of our own. Despite the workings of sinful men and women against us, they have no true power over us. The sins of those who do not repent and believe in Christ will be counted and held against them, condemning them to hell on the Last Day. The only fear we need have is the fear of falling away from God, of rejecting His love and His gracious gifts of forgiveness and eternal life. Always relying on God in faith, we, too, like John, will rise to the head of our class.

BONUS FEATURES

A little too much off the top: Whether it takes one swing or three swings, an axe, a sword, or a guillotine, beheading holds a special place in the hearts of executioners and the public because of the spectacle and unquestionable finality of it. Even if the bodies twitch or the eyes move for a moment or two afterward, everyone knows there is no coming back.

While the French Revolution is the place and time best known for beheadings, no one mastered the art of decapitation quite like the English, whose monarchs sent heads rolling for centuries. Henry VIII's wives Anne Boleyn and Katherine Howard stand at the front of a long line of tops the English cropped. But don't think other nations didn't have deadhead fun too.

William Wallace: Scottish hero for whom King Edward I of England felt distinct hatred. Prior to his beheading in 1305, Wallace was hanged, drawn and quartered, and eviscerated (his intestines and such cut out) while he still lived. After his beheading, he was cut into pieces, and his head and limbs were displayed at separate places throughout Scotland.

Marie Antoinette: The naïve queen of France blamed for all the excesses of her times met the guillotine in 1793.

Robespierre: A key figure in the French Revolution's Reign of Terror, Robespierre argued for the execution of King Louis XVI and the trial of Marie Antoinette. He, himself, was overthrown and guillotined in 1794.

Imam Hussein: Hussein, the grandson of Muhammad, the founder of Islam, was surrounded with his army by enemy forces until his capture and beheading within his own tent. His death in AD 680 held major implications for the balance of political and religious power and is said to mark the division of Islam into Shiite and Sunni factions.

Blackbeard: The terrifying, most famous pirate of all died when a group of British sailors attacked him and his crew. He sustained a massive number of wounds before keeling over. He was beheaded after death so the leader of the victorious British could use the head to collect a bounty.

Cicero: This extremely influential Roman philosopher, politician, and linguist spread the belief that moral standards were more important than government law. A supporter of the idea of a republic in Rome, Cicero was decapitated in 43 BC by Marc Antony's men for being on the wrong side of a political mess.

Getting the right moves: If you want to learn more about dances of romance and flirting, exploring some of these styles could be a good place to start:

- Belly dancing
- Tango
- Flamenco
- O'te'a
- Salsa
- Rumba
- Waltz

CHAPTER 15

HANGING ON TO GUILT

Who died: Judas

How he died: Hanged himself

Why he died: Despondency and lack of faith

When: AD 33, the year that Emperor Guangwu of China began fighting against the Rebellion of Gongsun Shu

Where in Scripture: Matthew 27:3–10 (also Acts 1:15–20)

A bad kisser? Most people with love on their minds would hate to have those words spoken about them. Today's story features someone whose kiss was terrible for altogether different reasons.

Forget the latest sitcom romance or royal wedding. Apart from fairy tales and fiction, this is probably the most famous kiss of all time, which is amazing because no one woke up from a deep sleep, no frogs turned into princes, and no true love was revealed. Instead, the Prince of Peace was turned over to soldiers and corrupt religious leaders to be judged, while the disciples hopped away in terror of being caught as well. And the kiss had little to do with love of any sort. Meanwhile, the kisser himself, Judas Iscariot, felt like he'd just kissed a lemon, souring soon after on the whole experience.

Up to that moment, he'd been confident enough to mess up everything he'd devoted himself to the last few years. He'd thought it would be worth it for the money and the connections it would bring. Instead, the money didn't matter any more, his new friends despised him, and he realized that some mistakes simply couldn't be undone.

It seemed unthinkable that someone who spent so much time up close in the company of God's Son could do that. He'd been one of Jesus' closest friends. How did this happen? While we're never told much about Judas, it's worth taking a step back for an insight or two into what happened before this historic betrayal—before the worst kiss ever.

FOLLOWER FLASHBACK

Judas Iscariot is one of those disciples whose backstory is a mystery. Even his calling by Jesus to be a disciple is not in the Bible. He simply appears on the lists along with the other eleven. He's not even the only Judas. The other Judas, also called Thaddeus, was even defined by who he wasn't: "Judas (not Iscariot)" (John 14:22). While he shared the name, there would be no confusing him with the traitor.

Like the other disciples, Judas was called by Jesus and spent years traveling with Him, learning from Him, and witnessing Him perform miracle

THAT REMINDS ME: LONG BEFORE THE EVENTS OF HOLY WEEK, PETER GAVE JUDAS THE CLUE HE NEEDED TO RECEIVE FAITH AND SALVATION WHEN HE SAID, "LORD, TO WHOM SHALL WE GO? YOU HAVE THE WORDS OF ETERNAL LIFE" (JOHN 6:68). YET, STILL, JUDAS FOCUSED ON THIS WORLD AND NOT ON THE WORLD TO COME. IT'S FITTING THEN THAT IN THE SAME CONVERSION, JESUS SAID, "DID I NOT CHOOSE YOU, THE TWELVE? AND YET ONE OF YOU IS A DEVIL" (V. 70).

after miracle. Along with the other disciples, Judas was given authority by Jesus to drive out unclean spirits and to heal.

After all that, if Judas didn't know that Jesus was God's Son, he at least knew that Jesus was powerful, kind, and blessed by God.

Judas had been given a position of responsibility among the Twelve. He was the treasurer, an important role for taking care of the poor and for keeping the group fed and cared for, since Jesus didn't create miraculous meals every day. That Matthew the tax collector is not the treasurer either testifies that Judas was extremely good with money or that it was better to separate Matthew from the temptation and the perception of misbehavior—since tax collectors of the time were seen as corrupt. Either way, in the end, it was Judas's focus on the material world that led him astray.

Judas first showed his true colors at Bethany. When Martha's sister, Mary, lovingly anointed Jesus' feet with a pound of expensive ointment, Judas questioned why it wasn't sold to feed the poor. And the text itself reveals that Judas didn't care one lick about the poor but was upset because he stole from the group's money. If Mary had sold the ointment, there would have been more for him to steal. Not even mentioning this motive, but instead alluding to His own death, Jesus rebuked Judas sharply.

Whatever was happening until this point, it seems that this was the final straw for Judas. Perhaps he finally realized that Jesus was not the kind of Messiah he thought Him to be. Jesus wasn't going to be a rich and powerful earthly king who would reward His friends.

JUST WONDERING: YOU'D THINK AFTER SO MUCH TIME TOGETHER, JUDAS WOULD HAVE CLOSE FRIENDS AMONG THE DISCIPLES. HOWEVER, OF THE TWELVE, JUDAS WAS THE ONLY ONE WHO WASN'T A GALILEAN. DO YOU THINK BEING AN OUTSIDER SEPARATED HIM FROM THE OTHERS? WHAT DO YOU IMAGINE JUDAS EXPECTED TO DO AFTER HIS BETRAYAL OF JESUS?

Was there more to it than this? Most certainly. People are complex, as are their motives. What we know is that two of the Gospels tell us that immediately after the ointment episode, Judas went to the chief priests to see what they'd give him for Jesus. They offered thirty big pieces of silver, which apparently was enough, because from then on Judas was itching to find the right moment to betray his friend.

DECEITFUL LIPS

Judas didn't have to wait long. Within the week, he was sitting with the other disciples and Jesus celebrating the Passover. Judas was feeling pretty confident. He'd made arrangements already with the priests, and there was no chance that Jesus or the other disciples would catch on.

That's when Jesus announced out of the blue that one of them would betray Him. Judas's hands were surely sweating at that point. And when Jesus point-blank called him out to Peter, Judas knew he had to act fast—a thought Jesus agreed with as He said, "What you are going to do, do quickly"

JUST WONDERING: TWO PLACES IN THE GOSPELS SAY THAT "SATAN ENTERED INTO JUDAS" (LUKE 22:3; JOHN 13:27). THIS DOES NOT MEAN THAT JUDAS WASN'T ACCOUNTABLE FOR HIS ACTIONS. SATAN WAS THE MOTIVATING FORCE, BUT JUDAS IS THE ONE WHO ACTED AS TRAITOR TO CHRIST. WHAT DOES IT MEAN WHEN SOMEONE SAYS, "THE DEVIL MADE ME DO IT"? HOW IS THAT STATEMENT BOTH TRUE AND FALSE?

(John 13:27). Judas hurried away from the table while the other disciples probably thought he was going out to buy stuff.

Even then, Judas could have changed his mind and backed out of his plans. It's not like the chief priests could confront Judas publicly without revealing their own secret scheming. However, Judas stayed resolute.

It wasn't hard for Judas to figure out where to lead the soldiers and the other musclemen the chief priests had provided for him. The Garden of Gethsemane was one of Jesus' favorite places to go with His group. Since it was dark, Judas approached first to give Jesus a kiss of greeting—a sign of respect—making it clear which guy was the soldiers' target. Even as Judas approached with a "Hiya, Rabbi," Jesus gave him yet another chance to turn aside, saying, "Judas, would you betray the Son of Man with a kiss?" (Luke 22:48). A moment later, Judas answered the question silently.

Proverbs 12:13 says, "An evil man is ensnared by the transgression of his lips," something that happened to Judas without him needing to speak a single word. Always kind, Jesus again called Judas a friend and made it clear that betraying Him was a conscious decision. Judas could have no doubts that Jesus knew what was happening.

Right then, the soldiers swooped in, and, after Peter fought a brief fight, the disciples sprinted away, and Jesus was arrested. We don't hear another word about Judas until his end, but it's safe to assume that he was given access to see much of what happened during Jesus' trials. Even as they led Jesus away to Pilate, before the final sentence had been passed, Judas knew what the leaders had in mind for Jesus. He knew that Jesus would be crucified.

A DESPAIRING HEART

At that point, a switch was flipped in Judas, and he changed his mind. He regretted his betrayal of Jesus and desperately wanted to take it back. What specifically triggered this change of heart is unclear. It could have been words spoken by Jesus before Caiaphas, watching others spit on and strike Jesus, a memory of their time together, or the cold, hard reality that his betrayal would result in Jesus' death.

The reason doesn't matter, just as Judas's regret didn't matter to the chief priests and elders when he brought the thirty pieces of silver back, trying to undo the bargain or at least rid himself of the evidence. They all but laughed when he said, "I have sinned by betraying innocent blood" (Matthew 27:4).

Judas threw the money into the temple and left the priests, who took the money and bought a burial place for strangers since it wasn't lawful to put this blood money in the treasury. It's laughable that after their efforts to push, prod, and quietly break the rules and regulations of society and the demands of the Law they should care about being "lawful."

Judas, however, didn't care what they did with it. His mind was set on only one thing: he had betrayed Jesus, a man sent by God, a miracle worker for the masses, a friend who had loved Judas even while Judas was betraying Him. Judas could see only his own failure, only his "unforgivable" sin. How we long for Judas to catch a sidelong glance from Jesus at this point, to have Jesus mouth the words "I forgive you," and to have Judas realize that the words truly applied to him. But in Judas's state of guilty self-inspection,

THAT REMINDS ME: ROMANS 5:8 SAYS, "GOD SHOWS HIS LOVE FOR US IN THAT WHILE WE WERE STILL SINNERS, CHRIST DIED FOR US." JUDAS WAS IN THE SAME BOAT AS EVERY OTHER MEMBER OF THE HUMAN RACE. HE WAS A SINNER. A SINGLE SIN—AND IT DOESN'T MATTER WHAT SIN—IS ENOUGH TO SEPARATE A PERSON FROM GOD. BUT THE FORGIVENESS CHRIST DIED TO EARN WAS JUST AS MUCH FOR JUDAS AS IT IS FOR US TODAY. THE DIFFERENCE BETWEEN JUDAS AND US IS OUR FAITH THAT BELIEVES THIS GIFT IS TRUE AND RECEIVES IT. JUDAS HAD NO SUCH FAITH.

even a face-to-face conversation would have mattered little. He did not have faith in who Jesus was and the most important thing He could do: forgive the sins of anyone, even Judas.

In that position, it's no wonder that Judas's solution was suicidal despair. Matthew simply tells us that Judas hanged himself. In Acts, Peter goes into more detail, explaining that Judas hanged himself in the very field the priests would purchase with the silver. Further, there was nothing peaceful about his death, for the rope broke and "falling headlong he burst open in the middle and all his bowels gushed out" (Acts 1:18). While it's possible there was such a steep spot or jagged rocks near his hanging for him to burst open like that, it's far more likely his corpse had been hanging by the neck for a while, rotting and bloating.

Contrary to what appears in many cinematic hangings, most hangings, especially suicides, don't end in a quick broken neck. Instead, the noose strangles the neck, pulled tighter by the weight of the person's own body. This cuts off both the air supply to the lungs and the blood supply to the brain. No oxygen is received, and the person asphyxiates, struggling for that last breath. The pressure on the neck can also result in a fatal heart attack. It can take several excruciatingly long minutes for unconsciousness to set in and twenty or so minutes for death to occur.

Judas made sure he would die in way that was painful and shameful. Scripture tells us that everyone knew what had happened to him afterward and knew about the place where he hanged himself.

WHY IS THIS IN THE BIBLE?

Judas is the mirror opposite of the thief on the cross who teaches us that even those who have nothing can be saved. Judas's lesson is that even those who seem to have it all in the Church can fall away.

Luke 6:16 mentions, "Judas, who became a traitor," implying that Judas did not begin this way. There wasn't a long-planned conspiracy to plant him as a spy who would befriend and then turn on Jesus at an opportune moment. Contrary to scholars who reinterpret Scripture, neither was Judas pretending to be a traitor at Jesus' own urging so as to make the necessary crucifixion happen. Judas did what he did, and he took full ownership of his terrible deeds.

Sadly, he never reached the next step of asking God to take the burden from him, to forgive him. He never realized that even a betrayal as great as his could be forgiven. Despite traveling with Jesus and hearing His words, he'd missed the point of His ministry after all. He'd missed all those stories of lost sheep, lost coins, and lost sons. He'd missed Jesus saying that the righteous do not need forgiveness, but sinners do. He'd missed Jesus' outreach to prostitutes, crooks, foreigners, and every manner of lowlife. These were the ones, the lost, that Christ had come for. And Judas never put it together that this was exactly what he was: lost.

Has a soul ever been so lost as his, so misguided? The story of Judas's repentance and forgiveness could have put Peter's dramatic denial and reinstatement to shame. Judas could have been the greatest symbol of undeserved mercy and love of all time. But, instead, he closed his heart to all but despair. The Law had done its work in him so well that there was no space left for the Gospel. And he didn't wait around to see the happy ending for us all and for the One he had betrayed.

Faithful preachers of God's Word will tell you that the Law alone cannot save. It does not drive sinners to hope that there's a way out, but to repentance. While repentance is much to be desired, it is useless to one's salvation without faith that God is both willing and capable of forgiving one's sins. Through the story of Judas—and the story of Peter, whose betrayal is forgiven—we are urged to trust in the forgiveness Christ earned for us on the cross and believe that we poor sinners are exactly the people He wishes to forgive.

BONUS FEATURES

Famous traitors:

Marcus Junius Brutus the Younger is best known to most people from Shakespeare's play *Julius Caesar.* Brutus was a noble man and a nobleman who, despite being treated kindly by and sharing a close relationship with Caesar, joined the assassination plot against him that resulted in Caesar being stabbed to death.

Guy Fawkes has an interesting place in history because traitors don't usually get their own parties complete with fireworks, but Guy Fawkes does. Each year in England, November 5 is a commemoration of the thwarting of the treacherous plan of Guy Fawkes and his co-conspirators to blow up King James I and Parliament with thirty-six barrels of gunpowder. Sentenced to be hanged and drawn and quartered, Fawkes leapt to his death instead.

Robert Ford shot his personal hero, mentor, and gang leader, Jesse James, in the head to collect a bounty. James had trusted Ford and his brother as the only surviving members of his gang. Despite being promised a $10,000 reward, the Fords received only $500 and were almost hanged.

Benedict Arnold was a talented commander of the American Revolution, responsible, at least in part, for several key victories. However, since he wasn't the easiest guy to get along with, he did not receive the credit he deserved. Feeling unappreciated, he offered to sell West Point to the British, but the plan was discovered before the deal was done. He switched sides but is said to have greatly regretted his actions later in life.

Mir Jafar, a commander in Bengal's army, made a deal with the British to stay out of the way so they could depose the country's ruler. Jafar did, they did, and in return he was made ruler of Bengal. He was, however, a puppet ruler, obliged to do everything the British ordered him to do. His betrayal paved the way for two hundred years of British rule.

A kiss is still a kiss: Fortunately, most of the time, the word *kiss* inspires not thoughts of betrayal but happiness. Whether your next kiss is for your mom, your grandma, or the trophy you'll win after the big game, here's how you can call it a kiss in other words.

English: *kiss*
Swahili: *busu*
Swedish: *kyss*
French: *bisou*
Dutch: *kus*
Afrikaans: *soen*
Italian: *bacio*
Basque: *musu*
Spanish: *beso*
Czech: *polibek*
Hebrew: הָקִישְׁנ
Greek: φιλί
Vietnamese: *hôn*
Latin: *oscula*

CHAPTER 16

THE TERRIBLE TREE

Who died: Jesus

How He died: Crucifixion

Why He died: Sacrifice for world's sins

When: AD 33, the year that Roman Emperor Tiberius founded a credit bank in Rome

Where in Scripture: Matthew 27; Mark 15; Luke 23; and John 19

Ladies and gentlemen, step right up to history's favorite game show: *Who Is Jesus?* Kings and slaves, wise guys and fools, scientists and theologians, and pretty much everyone in between has asked this question at one time or another: Who is Jesus?

They were asking that question before He was born, before He was in His mother's womb. From the time of Adam and Eve, people have wondered, "Exactly who is this Savior, this Messiah? What does Messiah even mean?" And for centuries and centuries until His birth, they kept asking.

You'd think His birth, His life, His death, and His resurrection, documented nicely in four Gospel books, would put an end to the discussion, but, if anything, the questions have become louder. Today, even in Christian churches, countless people ask, "Who is Jesus?"

And that is a great question to ask because Jesus answers more questions than any person who has ever lived. He is the answer, and once we figure out the flaws with many of our questions, we'll see that He's the only answer that our hope for eternal life will ever need.

THAT REMINDS ME: JESUS IS NOT ONLY THE ANSWER TO OUR QUESTIONS, BUT HE IS ALSO THE FULFILLMENT OF GOD'S PROMISES. WE HEAR ABOUT THIS IN 2 CORINTHIANS 1:20: "FOR ALL THE PROMISES OF GOD FIND THEIR YES IN [JESUS]." YOU NEVER HAVE TO WONDER IF GOD WILL KEEP HIS PROMISES. THE ANSWER IS YES!

HOW WILL THIS BE?

Mary asked this question of the angel when she was told that she would have a child, for Mary was a virgin. The angel's answer echoes through the rest of the New Testament. It would be a miracle of the Holy Spirit, and the child would be the Son of God. This is key for understanding anything about Jesus. He is Mary's Son. He is God's Son. He is a human being. He is God. He is mortal and immortal. He is limited and He is all knowing and almighty.

The rest of Jesus' life and ministry was a balance between displays of His human nature and His divine nature. Along the way, most people saw Him as primarily one or the other. They saw either what they expected or what they needed Him to be. In Nazareth, the people He'd grown up around asked, "Is not this Joseph's son?" (Luke 4:22), and when He explained that He was far more than that, they attempted to stone Him.

Many of the people He ministered to focused on His divine nature, His miracle working. They wisely sought His help and healing to the degree that He exhausted His human body and needed time away to rest. But perhaps the greatest misunderstandings came when people tried to manipulate Him into proving His divine power at a time of their choosing, rather than allowing Him to serve how and when He saw fit. Some of these requests, such as His mother's at the wedding in Cana, were innocent.

Others were offered more as threats, such as in Luke 23:6–12, when Herod was eager to see a miraculous sign, and not receiving one, he mocked Jesus and sent Him along the path to final judgment. Soon, Pilate would ask Him, "Are You the King of the Jews? (John 18:33), and Jesus tells him shortly that His "kingdom is not of this world" (v. 36).

WHO DO YOU SAY THAT I AM?

As the Passion Narrative—the suffering and death of Jesus—unfolded, Jesus' human nature exhibited more and more prominence. From His blood-like sweat in the Garden of Gethsemane to the crown of thorns poking into His head to the nearly fatal lashing from the Roman soldiers, Jesus took it all like a man—for everyone would expect God to respond by blasting the offenders or at least defending Himself. By the time Jesus was staggering under the weight of the crossbeam and stumbling to His knees, the end was near. He had already suffered extreme blood loss, blinding pain, hunger, de-hydration, fatigue, and likely organ damage. The crucifixion might not have been needed to kill Him at this point, but it sure would move death along.

As He was hanging on the cross, stripped of His clothes and with nails holding His wrists in place, the question He'd much earlier asked the disciples held more relevance than ever. "Who do you say that I am?" (Matthew 16:15) was not just a question for the disciples but for every person present at the cruci-fixion and for every one of us who judge His death as important. Peter's answer, "You are the Christ, the Son of the living God" (v. 16), is the answer that all of us should give. How hard was it, though, for those watching Him die, seeing Him behave nothing like they thought God or God's Son should behave, to believe that He was anything more than a good man? God dying made no sense to people who not only knew God as all powerful but who simply desired a military overthrow of their political overlords.

JUST WONDERING: DURING HIS EARTHLY MINISTRY, JESUS LOVED USING QUESTIONS AS A TOOL TO EITHER DRAW OUT ANSWERS FROM OTHERS OR TO INTRODUCE TOPICS. HE HIMSELF WOULD OFTEN ANSWER HIS OWN QUESTIONS. HE ALSO FOUND THAT QUESTIONS TIED WELL WITH PARABLES, GIVING PEOPLE SOMETHING CONCRETE TO LATCH ONTO BEFORE HE GUIDED THEM INTO GIVING THE ANSWER THEMSELVES.

How about for people today—is the answer still difficult? It is, so much so that we respond with a series of our own questions: Why couldn't He find another way? If He was dying for everyone, why couldn't He force people to believe? Why does He still allow suffering? Wouldn't a demonstration of His godly power have convinced more people? And for every answer received, more questions are generated.

Although some seek a God who can answer their questions, others see their questions as their god. They will believe in the impossible only if their minds and their thoughts can explain it. This means they will deny the impossible completely. God dying on the cross for man serves no purpose for people who don't believe in true sin. In this mindset, it's up to you. You're only sinful, they say, if you think you're sinful.

But we know better. We know who is sinful. Us. And we know who He is. Jesus Christ, the self-sacrificing Son of God.

WHY HAVE YOU FORSAKEN ME?

If we think our questions are difficult to handle, try on the question Jesus asked His Father in Matthew 27:46: "My God, My God, why have

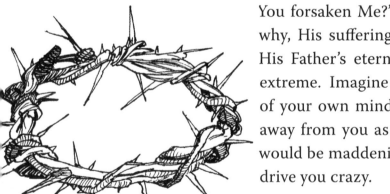

You forsaken Me?" Even though Jesus knew why, His suffering at being separated from His Father's eternal peaceful presence was extreme. Imagine having parts of yourself, of your own mind and body, suddenly shut away from you as if they'd never existed. It would be maddening, as in, it would literally drive you crazy.

And this happened as Jesus' physical, mental, and emotional exhaustion peaked. He was hungry, thirsty, anemic, publicly humiliated, bruised, exhausted, and suffering failure of His body systems. In this state, He was abandoned by His Father. At His Baptism, Christ was baptized into our sins. He bore these through His sinless life, and now they rested on His shoulders alone as He hung alone. As mockers in the crowd said unknowingly, He actually could have climbed off that cross, relieved all the pain, and punished all the offenders.

Instead, He faced hell on that cross. Hell was separation from God, from all the benefits of His gracious will, from His kindness shining on Him in the smallest ways. Hell is a place of suffering, and how could any suffering be greater than what He was experiencing?

JUST WONDERING: SATAN MANIPULATED WELL TO MOVE THE PRIESTS, PILATE, AND JUDAS INTO THE RIGHT PLACES WITH THE RIGHT LIES WHISPERED IN THEIR EARS. HE THOUGHT CHRIST'S DEATH WOULD VERIFY THAT THE WORLD HAD BEEN PLACED EVEN MORE STRONGLY IN HIS CONTROL. WHEN DID SATAN REALIZE HIS MISTAKE AND UNDERSTAND THAT CHRIST WAS DEFEATING HIM AND SIN ON THE CROSS? WAS IT WHILE LISTENING TO ONE OF CHRIST'S SAYINGS FROM THE CROSS OR DURING HIS VICTORY VISIT TO HELL WHILE IN HIS TOMB?

While His heart and kidneys headed toward failure, Jesus had to pull up against the nails through His feet and wrists to allow Himself to inhale properly. Every breath, then, brought on more pain and more exhaustion. His slow asphyxiation—the depletion of oxygen to His brain and body—was nearing its end. The punishments He'd suffered earlier were shortening His time on the cross from days to mere hours.

So why did the loving Father forsake His only-begotten Son? Because He had to. Because letting Christ bear our sins alone and suffer hell was the only way He could fulfill the punishment our sins had earned. Only in this way would our sins be paid in full and we would be rescued from eternal suffering in hell ourselves. And when the task was completed, He cried out, "It is finished" (John 19:30). Then He committed His soul into His Father's hands, bowed His head, and died.

A thrust of a soldier's spear into Jesus' side, into His lungs and heart, verified that He was dead.

THAT REMINDS ME: ISAIAH 53 IS A BEAUTIFUL CHAPTER THAT HAS MUCH TO SAY ABOUT CHRIST'S WORK FOR US, INCLUDING THIS: "HE WAS PIERCED FOR OUR TRANSGRESSIONS; HE WAS CRUSHED FOR OUR INIQUITIES; UPON HIM WAS THE CHASTISEMENT THAT BROUGHT US PEACE, AND WITH HIS WOUNDS WE ARE HEALED" (V. 5).

From there, His body was taken away by Joseph of Arimathea and Nicodemus, buried in a tomb, and left as the Sabbath began.

WHY IS THIS IN THE BIBLE?

If you wonder at all the suffering of the crucifixion and torment followed by torment, they are recorded so it is clear that Christ really, truly did die for the sins of the world. They are recorded so that His resurrection from the dead doesn't seem like a trick or a medical mistake. He was fully dead. And on the third day, on Easter, Jesus became fully alive again. The third and final enemy, death, was defeated as well, tying us eternally to His new life in heaven.

Without the account of Christ's death on the cross, the Bible would be nothing but a helpful history of the Jewish people, a recollection of a national deity protecting His people in days of old. In short, the book would not mean anything for us in this life or the next. We'd know a tale of the world's creation and fall into sin, but there would be no reason to believe it, for there would be no God waiting around to help us and preserve us.

Christ's death and resurrection are everything to the Bible, just as they are everything to the Christian. His suffering was real, showing the darkness of our sin. His death was real, showing the bitterness of what we deserved in His place. His resurrection was real, showing that our resurrection on the Last Day will be real as well. We are not helpless and hopeless. We have a God who hung around after creation to continue caring for us and who provided the ultimate solution with the sacrifice of His own Son.

Who is He? The only One who matters. Why did He die for us? Because He loves us. What must we do to be saved? Believe in Him for eternal life. Who is He? The Suffering Servant, the Christ, the Messiah, the Lamb of God, the King of the Universe, Jesus!

BONUS FEATURES

Chosen ones: Christ figures are everywhere in literature. These are characters whose stories in several ways parallel the story of Jesus. They might experience a personal betrayal, perform "miraculous" deeds, show great love and forgiveness, fight for what's right, and, especially, sacrifice themselves for the good of others. Often, they even rise again—or otherwise evade death. While there are thousands of these and all are not intentional Christs by the authors, here are a number of Christ figures in literature:

Aslan: The Chronicles of Narnia series
Santiago: *The Old Man and the Sea*
Gandalf and Frodo and Aragorn: *The Lord of the Rings*
Jim Conklin: *The Red Badge of Courage*
Atticus Finch: *To Kill a Mockingbird*
Gregor the Overlander: The Underland Chronicles
Harry Potter: The Harry Potter series
Simon: *Lord of the Flies*
Hazel: *Watership Down*
Sydney Carton: *A Tale of Two Cities*

Name that Savior: Jesus has so many different names and titles that they're almost impossible to count. But here are a few to get you started:

King of the Jews	Lord of glory	The Way
The Second Adam	Cornerstone	The Truth
Alpha and Omega	Prince of Peace	The Life
Son of God	Immanuel	Rock
Son of Man	King of kings	Advocate
Christ	Lion of Judah	Light of the World
Messiah	Man of Sorrows	Lamb
King of glory	Mediator	The Word
Good Shepherd	Redeemer	Suffering Servant

CHAPTER 17

ROCKED TO A PEACEFUL SLEEP

Who died: Stephen

How he died: Stoning

Why he died: Speaking the Gospel

When: AD 35, the year Tiridates III was appointed king of Parthia (he reigned only one year before being driven out)

Where in Scripture: Acts 6–7

It's hard not to take being stoned personally. Even though the stoners usually try to hide behind the shield of an impersonal mob, the person being stoned is not simply chosen at random. The stoned one is not given a quick or painless death. And it most definitely isn't an indifferent way to die. You'd feel each stone thrown, even the ones that miss. Intentionally or not, each person throwing is taking ownership of the final result. It's hard to feel loved when you're being stoned.

In part, that's because stoning is a community activity. It's the larger group's way of taking responsibility for driving evil out of their midst. As a method of execution, it was used in the Old Testament for serious offenses, such as adultery, witchcraft, and blasphemy. Some of the other stoning offenses may seem less significant to us, but they were critical to keeping good order and reverence for God. Stoning someone was never supposed to be an impulsive decision. It was to be an act of justice, not of anger.

So how did Stephen end up in front of a rock brigade? He was just supposed to be a deacon, someone who served the needs of the poor and hungry. Passing out food, helping widows find a place to stay, taking care of physical needs. How is it then that Stephen was killed for preaching a sermon? Wasn't that the apostles' job?

THE RIGHT MEN FOR THE JOB

The Early Christians in Jerusalem had one of those problems every church longs for: they were growing too fast. As a result, the apostles were stretched thin, not only preaching and teaching and performing miraculous signs, but also taking care of the widows and orphans, answering questions, and distributing food. Not that they didn't love all these tasks, but there was only so much they could accomplish in a day. To solve this problem, the followers of Christ gathered together and chose seven men with good reputations to especially take care of the physical needs of the poor and the widowed.

One of these men, Stephen, was particularly noted for being full of faith and the Holy Spirit. The Bible speaks of Stephen performing great wonders and signs—miracles—among the people. God's Word lived in him so strongly it could not help but come out. As a result, some of the people in the synagogue began to argue with him. His words, however, were from God, and he was so full of wisdom that they realized they had no chance of winning a religious debate with him. This, apparently, was too much for their pride

THAT REMINDS ME: ONE DETAIL THE STORY OF STEPHEN IS REMEMBERED FOR IS THE FIRST APPEARANCE OF SAUL IN THE BIBLE. A STUDENT OF THE PHARISEES, SAUL WAS A PASSIONATE DEFENDER OF GOD'S WORD AS HE UNDERSTOOD IT AND A PERSECUTOR OF CHRISTIANS. THE PROBLEM WAS THAT HE DIDN'T YET REALIZE THAT GOD'S WORD HAD JUST BEEN DEFINED IN THE PERSON AND WORK OF JESUS CHRIST. HIS UNDERSTANDING CHANGED WHEN JESUS APPEARED TO HIM ON THE ROAD TO DAMASCUS. FROM THEN ON, SAUL, WHO WOULD BE CALLED PAUL, DEDICATED HIS LIFE TO THE SAME SAVIOR STEPHEN HAD PROCLAIMED.

to bear, so much like what happened at Jesus' trial, that they prodded some men into lying about what Stephen had said so his words would sound like blasphemy.

Making sure the witnesses came along, Stephen's opponents in the synagogue hauled Stephen off to the Sanhedrin, the religious council, to accuse him. There, the witnesses twisted Stephen's words to sound like he was speaking against the temple and the customs and Law of Moses. This was a smart move that would appeal to multiple religious factions, since the Sadducees valued the temple most and the Pharisees held tightly to every detail of the law.

Yet even as they made their accusations against Stephen, "his face was like the face of an angel" (Acts 6:15), which must have been disturbing for some of these men. More disturbing to his listeners was what he said when the high priest asked him if the accusations were true.

IT'S SERMON TIME!

Stephen started speaking with respect, likely hooking them in with a discussion of Abraham and the patriarchs—always welcome topics for the Jewish religious authorities—but somewhere along the way he pulled a bait and switch on them. What began as a simple recounting of Jewish history soon made points that caused the council members to shift uncomfortably.

Even from the opening of his sermon, Stephen was opening doors they preferred not to look behind. He didn't just refer to Abraham, he referred to Abraham being called while living in another land, and rather than focusing on the importance of Canaan—the later Promised Land—Stephen noted that it wasn't a true home for Abraham.

Then, Stephen began talking about Isaac, Jacob, and Joseph, and that's when the zingers really started flying. As he revisited history, Stephen pulled up an old theme that the Book of Judges emphasized heartily: God kept raising heroes of the faith up to save His people from hardship, from their oppressors, and from slavery, and in response, the people rebelled against them and God. "Remember Moses," Stephen said. "Remember how while he was receiving the Law from God, the Israelites—your ancestors—made sacrifices to a golden calf."

Stephen was simultaneously teaching them and refuting the charges they made. While they said Stephen didn't care for the Law of Moses, it was really they who had turned their backs on much of the Law for generations. Stephen, on the other hand, was showing honor to the Law.

Stephen also deflected their other attack on him. They said he was attacking God's house, but Stephen pointed out that they were trying to make the temple into God's prison. He described how Solomon built a dwelling place for God, yet both Solomon and the prophet Isaiah explained how it was impossible for any dwelling built by human hands to fully contain God. However, the religious leaders on the council were, Stephen indirectly preached, honoring the building more than the One for whom it was built.

Closing his pointed speech, Stephen lined up his listeners with generations of Jews who resisted the Holy Spirit. "You're just as bad as your ancestors," Stephen insisted. Acts 7:52–53 ends with his words: "Which of the prophets did your fathers not persecute? And they killed those who announced beforehand the coming of the Righteous One, whom you have now betrayed and murdered, you who received the law as delivered by angels and did not keep it."

Basically, they killed the prophets. They killed John the Baptist. They killed Jesus. What gave them the right to act so full of themselves?

STONES AND THE ROCK

At Stephen's words, they were fuming and furious. Just picture a line of snorting bulls ready to charge. Then, Stephen, full of the Holy Spirit, looked up to heaven and saw the Jesus these people had killed standing at God's right hand. Of course, he told them what he saw.

So, prediction time, what do you think they did next?

    A. Pointed at the clouds and tried to find Jesus

    B. Asked Stephen who else he saw

    C. Charged at him yelling at the top of their lungs

You know the answer. They even covered their ears as they ran at him to make sure they wouldn't hear any more of his "heretical" words. The mob—this was no longer anything like a civilized trial—forced him out of the city and began throwing stones at him. And just to make sure they wouldn't dirty their good clothes, a young man named Saul watched the coats for them. "What good Jews," he likely thought as he watched them stone Stephen.

Stoning can be fast or slow. It can be extremely painful, or it can end with one well-thrown rock to the head that wipes out consciousness. We know nothing of how many bruises, broken bones, smashed facial features, or damaged organs Stephen suffered as a result of his stoning. What we do know is that he gladly followed in the steps of his forgiving Savior, calling out, "Lord Jesus, receive my spirit" (Luke 7:59). Then, falling to his knees, he cried out, "Lord, do not hold this sin against them" (v. 60). And the Bible says he fell asleep, at peace in the arms of the Lord.

JUST WONDERING: PERHAPS THE HARDEST WORDS EVER SPOKEN WERE THE WORDS STEPHEN ECHOED HERE, WHEN JESUS SAID, "FATHER, FORGIVE THEM, FOR THEY KNOW NOT WHAT THEY DO" (LUKE 23:34). IMAGINE SAYING THOSE WORDS TO YOUR GREATEST ENEMIES AT THE EXACT MOMENT WHEN THEY ARE DOING THE MEANEST THING THAT HAS EVER BEEN DONE TO YOU IN YOUR ENTIRE LIFE. HOW CAN YOU DEVELOP AN ATTITUDE THAT WILL ALLOW YOU TO NONJUDGMENTALLY, NONSARCASTICALLY SAY SUCH WORDS WHEN OTHERS OPPRESS YOU?

WHY IS THIS IN THE BIBLE?

"Precious in the sight of the LORD is the death of His saints" (Psalm 116:15). Just as Jesus' tears at the death of His friend Lazarus proved this point, so, too, does the death of Stephen. Why else would God allow him a vision of Jesus and the Father he was about to meet in person?

There were many saints in the Old Testament, believers in God's promise of a coming Messiah to save them from their sins. But it wasn't until Stephen that we see the first Christian death. In other words, this is the first death of someone who knows that Jesus suffered, died, and rose again for his sins. It's a pivotal moment in the life of the young Church. It's also an occurrence— the martyrdom, not the view of heaven—that would happen with increasing regularity in the years that followed.

What an example to all those who came after! Stephen spoke words of significance, unflinching in his faith, and called down forgiveness on his enemies. Is that not the very reason for the Church's existence? The Church is built to give forgiveness to those within it and to preach forgiveness to those outside it, urging them to join in and receive God's good and free gifts earned by the "Righteous One" (Acts 7:52) on the cross.

THAT REMINDS ME: IN GREEK, STEPHEN'S NAME MEANS "CROWN." WHAT A FITTING NAME FOR THE FIRST CHRISTIAN MARTYR, ESPECIALLY IN LIGHT OF REVELATION 2:10: "BE FAITHFUL UNTO DEATH, AND I WILL GIVE YOU THE CROWN OF LIFE."

But how exactly can one of the most violent deaths in the Bible be one of the most peaceful? That's the real mystery. The thought of discovering this answer for ourselves is terrifying, and, in our society, unlikely to be our experience. At the same time, we never know what circumstances might come our way. We never know what the world will throw at us and what words of faith we might need to speak in response. We do, however, know what Stephen did. God will supply all our needs and, in fact, He already has. The faith that God's Spirit grows within us draws us closer each day to the Savior who will never let us go it alone.

With His love within us, we need have no fear. He who stands at the right hand of the throne of God supports us with His arms, so that we may not stumble on our way to the day of our final sleep, as we await the glorious Last Day when our bodies and our praises shall rise for all eternity.

BONUS FEATURES

Reasons for stoning in the Old Testament: Stoning comes up a surprising amount in the Old Testament. It's one of the more common modes of execution, especially when a person or animal became unclean in a way that could not be cleansed. In such cases, stoning was both a punishment and a way of preserving the purity of the rest of the community. While there are likely others, here are a few of the crimes that earned stoning in Old Testament times:

- murder
- approaching Mount Sinai while God was there
- witchcraft and necromancy (using magic to speak to or summon the dead)
- consuming blood
- various sexual sins
- blaspheming God's name
- worshiping idols
- breaking the Sabbath (one man was gathering sticks on the Sabbath)
- cursing one's parents
- perjury (swearing something to be true that isn't)
- being an irredeemably stubborn and rebellious son

More martyrs: The history of the Church is packed with martyrs, people who died for their faith. While many of the tales not in Scripture come down to us only as tradition and are difficult if not impossible to verify, the sheer volume of them suggests that many are true in large part or hold major elements of what actually happened. We know, if nothing else, that many of these believers were painfully martyred, even if the manner of their deaths is uncertain. Here are a few of the traditional stories of martyrdom:

St. Lawrence: Thought to have known where secret hordes of treasure were held, Lawrence was given two days to bring all the "wealth of the Church" to the Emperor's palace. He showed up with the sick, the orphaned, and the widowed and declared, "These are the treasures of the Church." One tradition says he was slow-roasted on a grill for his impertinence, but another tradition says he was hanged.

St. Symphorosa: For refusing to offer sacrifices to pagan gods, this faithful mother was tied to a rock and thrown in a river. Her seven sons were then martyred in seven different ways.

St. Timothy and St. Maura: Timothy was imprisoned and tortured severely with heated metal rods for not handing over the Christian books he guarded. His wife, Maura, was brought in to break him, but she and he refused to cooperate. Although her fingers were cut off and her hair yanked out, she still professed her faith. They were crucified across from each other for ten days.

Polycarp: A disciple of the apostle John, old man Polycarp, the Bishop of Smyrna, was arrested and taken to the Roman Proconsul. There, he was given numerous promptings to turn from his faith and deny Jesus. Instead, Polycarp calmly rebutted every warning and threat with wisdom and wit, showing a rock-solid faith. Finally, he was burned alive while filled with prayers and thanks to God. Some say the fire itself did not burn him—that he had to be stabbed.

CHAPTER 18

THE WORM KING

Who died: Herod Agrippa I

How he died: Worms

Why he died: Hubris—thinking himself a god

When: AD 41, the year Emperor Caligula of Rome was assassinated and Emperor Claudius took his place

Where in Scripture: Acts 12

One true lesson that's seldom directly taught but is made very clear in Sunday School: there's no such thing as a good Herod. From killing the Bethlehem babies to backstabbing family members to beheading John the Baptist to persecuting Christians, the Herods were a nasty bunch.

In the case of this account's Herod, Herod Agrippa I, the grandson of the Herod who tried to kill baby Jesus, it wasn't just a single bad choice—it was a lifetime of evil spawned from a heritage of evil. And in a book that lingers on death, the Herods could have easily filled numerous chapters for the carnage they left in their immoral wake.

That doesn't mean the Herods were destined for such nasty deeds or that a heritage of corruption gave them no way out. The kings of Israel in the Old Testament showed there's more to it than DNA and family tradition: there are numerous bad kings coming from good, faith-filled fathers and numerous good kings coming from wicked fathers. It's something we still know: good apples can come from rotten trees, and rotten apples can come from strong trees. However, good is more likely to come from good, and bad is more likely to come from bad.

JUST WONDERING: ONE OF THE HARDEST QUESTIONS IN MORAL PHILOSOPHY IS HOW MUCH RESPONSIBILITY PARENTS SHOULD BEAR FOR THE ACTIONS OF THEIR CHILDREN—ESPECIALLY WHILE THEY'RE STILL YOUNG. WHAT DO YOU THINK? WHERE IS THE LINE BETWEEN HOLDING FAMILIES ACCOUNTABLE FOR THE CHILDREN THEY'VE RAISED AND HOLDING PEOPLE ACCOUNTABLE FOR THEIR OWN ACTIONS? WHY CAN A LEGACY OF BAD BEHAVIOR BE SO HARD TO ESCAPE?

So, before going further into this account, it's time for a little Herod 101.

HOW MANY HERODS DOES IT TAKE . . .

Trying to keep all the Herods straight in the New Testament can mess with your head. Just to make things a little easier, here's a summary of each one's biblical role, in order, and how they're related.

1. *Herod the Great* was a powerful non-Jewish king who not only tried to manipulate the Wise Men but also massacred the male infants in Bethlehem in an effort to kill Jesus. He also killed some of his own wives and children.

2. *Herod Archelaus* was a son of Herod the Great. He ruled half of his father's territory, including Judea and Samaria. Joseph avoided moving Mary and Jesus back from Egypt to Bethlehem because it was in this Herod's realm.

3. *Herod Antipas* was another son of Herod the Great, called "the Fox" by Jesus. He ruled Galilee and Perea. He divorced his first wife and married his brother's wife, Herodias. He had John the Baptist beheaded. Pilate sent Jesus to see him as part of Jesus' trial, and he was miffed because Jesus wouldn't perform a miracle for him.

4. *Herod Philip the Tetrarch* was another son of Herod the Great. He ruled an area north and east of Galilee. He married his niece, Salome, the girl who danced for John the Baptist's head.

5. *Herod Agrippa I* was the grandson of Herod the Great; he ruled a large territory and had an even larger ego. He killed James (brother of John) and arrested Peter. He also had a problem with worms. He's the victim of this chapter's gory death.

6. *Herod Agrippa II* was the son of Herod Agrippa I. The ruler of a large territory, he interviewed Paul along with Festus when Paul was imprisoned in Caesarea. Agrippa II wanted to set Paul free but couldn't because Paul had appealed to Caesar. If any of the Herods could be considered "good" or at least "not so bad," perhaps it would be him.

The Herods were obsessed with power and with one-upping members of their own family. They were willing to be underlings of Rome because they got their piece of the pie and could indulge their own greedy and violent desires.

GETTING AGRIPPA ON THE SITUATION

The Christian Church had begun making power moves, with Peter and others traveling about spreading the Word, Gentiles being baptized, and Paul and Barnabas just getting started. Many of the Jews were afraid of this new movement and what it would mean for their families and communities. Herod Agrippa I, sensing this, started playing rough with the Christians, violently oppressing them. Then, when he had James, the brother of John, killed with a sword, the Jews were thrilled.

"That's *it!*" thought Herod. The people wanted blood. At once, he arrested Peter, too, intending to bring him before the people after Passover. Then, they could have their fun beating and abusing him publicly before killing him. And Herod knew he would get all the praise. Excellent!

Unfortunately for Herod, God wasn't cool with his plan. The night before Herod was going to bring Peter out for all the torturous fun, an angel set Peter free of his chains and his guards, and led him out into the

THAT REMINDS ME: NOT COUNTING JUDAS, WHO ABANDONED HIS RIGHTS AS AN APOSTLE, JAMES IS THE FIRST OF THE TWELVE TO DIE AND THE ONLY ONE WHOSE DEATH IS RECORDED IN SCRIPTURE. BY CONTRAST, HIS YOUNGER BROTHER, JOHN, WAS THE LAST OF THE APOSTLES ALIVE AND IS REPUTED TO HAVE DIED A NATURAL DEATH AT AN OLD AGE.

city to freedom. When Herod found out the next day, he had the sentries put to death, even though it wasn't their fault.

Following that, Herod was angry with the people in a couple of his cities and probably punished them. So, eager to get back on his good side, they came to Herod begging for peace. He responded by putting on his finest royal robes, settling into his throne, and giving them a fancy speech, no doubt filled with expressions of his own greatness. Getting the hint of what was expected, the people went over the top praising Herod: "The voice of a god, and not of a man!" (Acts 12:22).

If Herod had even a scrap of humility or respect for God in him, he would have deflected, if not denied, this praise on the spot. Instead, he soaked it in. It was exactly the kind of thing he liked to hear. And for this sin of not giving the glory to God, an angel of the Lord immediately struck Herod down. But this wasn't a simple smiting dead on the spot. Instead, Herod was killed from the inside out, eaten by worms until his body stopped working.

THAT REMINDS ME: HEROD AGRIPPA I WAS NOT THE FIRST KING TO RECEIVE A PAINFUL DEATH IN EXCHANGE FOR HIS SINS AGAINST GOD. A SIMILAR FIGURE IS KING JEHORAM OF JUDAH. WHILE HIS FATHER, JEHOSHAPHAT, HAD MADE MANY GODLY DECISIONS, JEHOSHAPHAT'S ALLIANCE WITH ISRAEL'S HOUSE OF AHAB SEEMED TO CORRUPT HIS OWN FAMILY. JEHORAM, WHO MARRIED AHAB'S DAUGHTER, COMMITTED WICKED ACTS, INCLUDING KILLING HIS OWN BROTHERS. AS PUNISHMENT, HE CONTRACTED A DISEASE THAT CAUSED HIS BOWELS TO COME OUT.

The Bible says nothing more, so we're left to speculate what kind of worms did the job and how exactly he perished. However, there are numerous worms that are parasitic in humans and several that grow quite long, causing blockages and other issues in the intestines. Whatever the particular culprit, there's no doubt that Herod's death was excruciating.

WHY IS THIS IN THE BIBLE?

The ancient Greeks liked to talk a lot about fatal flaws: the one thing about a person that would cause his or her doom. For them, the worst of all was hubris: a man trying to take the place of the gods. This is a perfect word for Herod Agrippa I, who had no problem with others putting him in the place of God.

This is actually all too common of a weakness. Just consider the First Commandment for a moment: "You will have no other gods before Me." While there are many invented deities, human beings, animals, philosophical causes, and material possessions that people make into false gods, there's no god people enjoy worshiping more than themselves.

It could be argued that every violation of the First Commandment involves hubris—honoring of self as more important than God. To even consider something else as a god above God, a person has to make a decision to elevate his or her own judgment above God's clearly communicated will. And at the moment you consider your opinion to be more important than God's, you're making a god of yourself. This account is a clear warning about this type of pride, but that's not all it is.

Herod's story also shows the futility of opposing God's will for His Church. While God certainly allows believers in the Church to experience suffering and even death, He makes it clear that He is the one in control. All the forces of evil cannot prevent the Word of God from being spread to all nations, as the early believers were in the process of doing. This is a comforting thought. God was, is, and ever will be in charge of our lives. Though we may not understand our hardships, His care and protection of our bodies and our souls will not cease.

The verse immediately after this Herod's death makes the real point. Despite the ambitions of men like Herod, "the word of God increased and multiplied" (Acts 12:24).

BONUS FEATURES

Worms and the human body: Many different kinds of worms and other parasites enjoy feasting on the human body. While pinworms, roundworms, whipworms, hookworms, and others can cause weight loss, anemia, intestinal blockage, and a host of other conditions, including death, there's just something about those incredibly long tapeworms that people find most fascinating.

Tapeworm facts:

- They commonly cause fun conditions like diarrhea, vomiting, and loss of appetite.

- They can be contracted through contaminated water and undercooked meat.

- They can't survive outside the host's body.

- They can migrate from one part of the body to another. They can live in intestines, brains, and eyes, among other places.

- Roughly twenty million people are infected with tapeworms.

- Typically six to thirty inches in length, they can grow to be twenty feet or longer.

- They can cause death by making the brain swell.

- People often don't realize they have tapeworms, and tapeworms can live for thirty years in a person.

- Some people intentionally ingest tapeworms to try to lose weight. (Note: This is a very bad idea. Don't do it!)

Deaths of the apostles: As mentioned earlier, the Bible tells us nothing of the exact fates of the apostles, apart from James and the suicidal Judas. It does, however, suggest that many would face suffering and unpleasant endings. While no other source should ever be put on a level with Scripture, some sources are more solid than others, so there is considerable tradition for how the rest of the apostles died. Furthermore, tradition states that all but one of them died martyrs' deaths. Of prime importance is not how they died, but what they died for: their faith in Jesus Christ.

- Simon Peter: crucified upside down in Rome
- James: killed by a sword at Herod's command
- John: died a natural death at an old age, though some say he was martyred as well
- Andrew: crucified on a transverse, or X-shaped, cross
- Philip: stoned to death while tied to a cross
- Bartholomew, a.k.a. Nathaniel: flayed (skinned) alive, then beheaded
- Matthew: stabbed in Ethiopia
- Thomas: killed with a spear in India
- James the son of Alphaeus: stoned and clubbed
- Judas, a.k.a. Jude, a.k.a. Thaddeus: perhaps killed by an axe
- Simon the Zealot: crucified or sawn in half
- Matthias (the replacement for Judas chosen by lot): stoned to death, then decapitated with an axe
- Paul (the replacement for Judas chosen by Christ): beheaded with a sword in Rome

A Few Last Thoughts on Death

By its nature, this book has spent most of its time on stories about people who died for their sinful choices, for their rebellions against God. That's not the only reason people die horrible deaths, though. Some are senseless, some are tragic, and some—the lucky ones?—die for their faith.

It's been said that one of the best ways to see the truth of what the apostles taught is to see what they were willing to suffer to defend it. If the resurrection was merely a fairy tale and Christ's suffering and death a lie they made up to gain influence and popularity, why would they cling to it to such extremes? More than that, they were willing to die for their faith. And not just quiet, painless deaths, but horrible, violent ends. This book is called *Gory Deaths* for a reason, and the deaths of the apostles and other martyrs of the Christian faith fit right in.

There's a reason so many have repeated the words of the Early Church Father Tertullian: "The blood of the martyrs is the seed of the Church." A faith that does not waver even in the face of death cannot help but inspire others to take that faith to heart.

Just take a look back at the Bonus Features in chapters 17 and 18, and try to pick one of those deaths you wouldn't mind enduring. It's something of a worst-hits mix of terrible ways to die. But like with any death in this book or in real life, that's not the part that matters most. What does matter is the true faith or stubborn disbelief that came before death and the eternal life or eternal suffering that will come after.

The wages of sin is death, and so it goes in this book. We live to die, and there is no way out save one. Despite what some poets might say, death is never pretty. When it is the death of one of His saints, it is, however, precious in the sight of the Lord. That, friends, is the message of this book. God longs for us to meet our earthly end as His saints. We don't earn this by good deeds and kind words, for they too often fail us. We don't earn it by holy prayers and devout thoughts, for sin always creeps its way in.

Rather, Jesus Christ, the conqueror of death, has earned salvation for us. He has earned eternal life for us. These gifts are given us by God that we might receive them gladly, repent fully, and realize forever how much we need what is offered. God is able to save. Death is not the end. And no matter how gory the details of our lives become, God's ability to forgive us is greater still.

You, His saints, claim the glory of the life that shatters death, the life that is now yours!

REFERENCES

In addition to Scripture, there were numerous other resources that were helpful to the development of this book. If you find yourself curious for more information, check these out to discover more interesting facts and thoughts. For the most part, the dates of Bible events were taken from *The Lutheran Study Bible*.

Alexander, David and Pat Alexander, eds. *Eerdmans Handbook to the Bible*. Grand Rapids, MI: Eerdmans, 1973, 1983.

Brownrigg, Ronald. *The Twelve Apostles*. New York: Macmillan, 1974.

Concordia Commentary Series. Assorted volumes. St. Louis: Concordia.

Coogan, Michael D., ed. *The Oxford History of the Biblical World*. New York: Oxford U.P., 1988.

Engelbrecht, Edward, ed. *Lutheran Bible Companion:* Vols. 1 and 2. St. Louis: Concordia, 2014.

Engelbrecht, Edward, ed. *The Lutheran Study Bible*. St Louis: Concordia, 2009.

Ferguson, George. *Signs and Symbols in Christian Art*. New York: Oxford U.P., 1958.

Franzmann, Werner H. *Bible History Commentary: Old Testament*. Milwaukee: WELS Board for Parish Education, 1980.

Inch, Morris. *12 Who Changed the World*. Nashville: Thomas Nelson, 2003.

Kretmann, Paul E. *Popular Commentary of the Bible: Old Testament* Vols. 1 and 2 and New Testament Vols. 1 and 2. St. Louis: Concordia, 1921–24.

Kugel, James L. *The Bible as It Was*. New York: Belknap Press, 1999.

Luther, Martin. *What Luther Says: A Practical In-Home Anthology for the Active Christian.* St. Louis: Concordia, 1959.

Luther's Small Catechism with Explanation. St. Louis: Concordia, 1986, 1991.

Stanley, Gerard Joseph, Sr. *He Was Crucified: Reflections on the Passion of Christ.* St. Louis: Concordia, 2009.

The People's Bible Commentary Series. Assorted Volumes. St. Louis: Concordia.

Vamosh, Miriam Feinberg. *Daily Life at the Time of Jesus.* Herzlia, Israel: Palphot Ltd, 2001.

Vos, Howard F. *Nelson's New Illustrated Bible Manners and Customs.* Nashville: Thomas Nelson, 1999.

Ward, Kaari, ed. *Jesus and His Times.* Pleasantville, NY: Reader's Digest Association, 1987.

ABOUT THE AUTHOR: Jonathan Schkade
lives in Jefferson City, Missouri, where he
works as an editor and author. He enjoys
reading, cooking, procrastinating, and staring
awestruck at his wife and daughters.

ABOUT THE ILLUSTRATOR: Gleisson Cipriano
is an illustrator and comic artist, working
from Bauru, in the countryside of São Paulo,
Brazil. Most of his time is invested in studying,
drawing, and consuming creative content.